STENA GALLOWAY

# Stena Line

## Irish Sea

innovation
and flexibility
– the key to success

John Bryant

The *Stena Edda* looks magnificent as she sets out from Weihai, China, to begin her sea trials, 5th September 2019. *(CMI Jinling Weihai Shipyard/Stena Line)*

# Contents

Published by
Ferry Publications
PO Box 33, Ramsey, Isle of Man, IM99 4LP
Tel; +44 (0) 1624 898446
www.ferrypubs.co.uk

In January 2020, the *Stena Superfast X* deputised during the *Stena Horizon*'s refit on the overnight Rosslare-Cherbourg route. She is seen here at the Irish port as the *Stena Europe* arrives from Fishguard. *(Gordon Hislip)*

4

# Introduction

Today, there is little doubt that Stena Line is 'The World's Leading Ferry Company', operating on 19 different routes criss-crossing the Baltic Sea, Scandinavia, North Sea and Irish Sea. Five of these links connect Great Britain with the Irish Republic and Northern Ireland revealing just how much the UK market relies on Stena Line. Its origins are surprisingly humble and can be traced back as far as the latter part of the 1930s when Sten A Olsson set up a business recycling metals for the shipbuilding industry based around Gothenburg. It was not until 1947 that he became a ship owner, utilising small coasters to carry scrap metal as well as other cargoes.

His entry into the world of ferries came in December 1962 when he chartered a small passenger ferry to serve on a route from Gothenburg to Skagen in Northern Denmark. From such modest beginnings and now almost 60 years on his company has grown into one of the largest and highly regarded ferry companies throughout Northern Europe.

Throughout its history Stena Line has long been in the forefront of ferry design and innovation, whether it be on the technical side in hull forms, machinery and vehicle capacities or in raising the bar when improving the on-board quality of the facilities and accommodation on offer. Sometimes things do not always turn out quite as planned as with the HSS, a victim of rising fuel prices coupled with business requiring a more balanced mix of freight and car traffic all year round. But what innovation! Stena's HSS concept put new life back into travelling and somehow with its demise the ferry world seemed a little less exciting. However, a new dawn is breaking as three vessels of the E-flexer class, *Stena Estrid* (Holyhead–Dublin), *Stena Edda* and *Stena Embla* (Birkenhead–Belfast) have just entered service (or are about to) on the Irish Sea, bringing new standards amid much excitement in these challenging times.

Whilst Scandinavia continued to be Stena's main area of focus, in the late 1980s they began to turn their attentions on operations to the UK. In June 1989 the company acquired the Zeeland Steamship Company's (Stoomvaart Maatschapij Zeelandia - SMZ) route from Hoek van Holland to Harwich and then in April 1990 took control of Sealink British Ferries from Sea Containers. This latter transaction was termed by some as 'hostile takeover' and was not without its issues. Sea Containers had invested relatively little money into new ships so what had been a reasonably modern shipping fleet when Sealink was privatised in 1984 was now beginning to age.

Whilst this book is primarily about Stena Line's Irish Sea history and successes today, the company's earlier ships were not unknown in UK waters mainly as a result of a number of short-term charters long before they purchased Sealink British Ferries. Two vessels which served on the Irish Sea routes are worth noting here as they radically changed the perceptions of those involved in railway operated shipping and of the public in general. The first was the diminutive *Stena Nordica* (1965), which from January 1966, was chartered by the Caledonian Steam Packet Company (a subsidiary of British Rail) for use on their services between Stranraer and Larne, continuing to so until to do so 1970. She was the first drive-through ferry to operate for British Rail, still bound by the inherent inertia of the railway establishment and continuing to build steam-powered stern loading car ferries. Despite her small size she could accommodate no less than 28 lorries or 120 cars on her vehicle deck. On the downside she did not have stabilisers, but she was a wake-up call, one which was heeded and manifested itself with their first diesel-powered drive-through ferry, the *Antrim Princess* in 1967.

Also worthy of mention was the *Stena Normandica* which

The *Stena Nordica* (1965) began her career marketed as 'The Londoner' sailing between Tilbury and Calais. In 1966 she was chartered to the Caledonian Steam Packet Company for services between Stranraer and Larne, becoming the first drive-through ship to serve for the British Railways Board. *(FotoFlite)*

With bow visor raised, the *Stena Normandica* cautiously approaches the ramp at Fishguard. *(Miles Cowsill)*

A well patronised *Stena Sea Lynx II* ready to depart from Holyhead for Dun Laoghaire in 1994. *(Gordon Hislip)*

The spectacular *Stena Explorer* begins to pick up speed as she exits the confines of the inner harbour at Holyhead on another 99 minute dash to Dun Laoghaire in August 1996. *(John Bryant)*

served on the southern corridor of the Irish Sea from Fishguard to Rosslare. She dated from 1974 and had previously seen service in short term charters around the east and south coasts of England. In 1979, she took up an extended charter for Sealink on the Fishguard route, initially for 19 months, but remained there until the end of 1989. Rather box-like in appearance but with comfortable provision for up to 1,400 passengers, it was her ability to carry up to 116 trailers or 470 cars on two full height vehicle decks that made her a game changer on the Irish Sea.

Today, with 30 years of gradual consolidation across their Irish Sea routes, Stena Line are now the dominant operator with services from Scotland, England and Wales to Northern Ireland and Ireland, not forgetting one from the latter country to Cherbourg in France. This success has been achieved through the acquisition or modification of routes according to demand and by introducing innovative new craft such as the HSS, whilst at the same time the judicious upgrading of existing tonnage making it fit for the challenges ahead.

Additionally, Stena's reputation of being able to acquire tonnage from other operators and to mould them into highly efficient and successful units, e.g. *Stena Superfast VII* and *Stena Superfast VIII* on their Cairnryan to Belfast service, continues to pay dividends.

As we enter the third decade of this century we see three more game changers come onto the scene in the form of the state-of-the-art eco-friendly vessels of the E-Flexer class, *Stena Estrid* (Holyhead - Dublin), *Stena Edda* and *Stena Embla* (Birkenhead - Belfast). With these superb ferries Stena Line has brought a new dimension to Irish Sea travel which will further consolidate their position in the market. Stena Line's mission statement '*Connecting Europe for a Sustainable Future*' is now rapidly coming to fruition.

Rather than chart the whole of the 150-year plus story this book picks up the thread for the Irish Sea railway services around the early 1960s just at the time Stena Line came into being in Scandinavia.

ONE

# The Inheritance

S tena Line, as a ferry company, began operations in Scandinavia nearly 60 years ago in 1962. Their activities on the Irish Sea have spanned for approximately for half of that time as in 2020 they celebrated 30 years of service. The Irish Sea inheritance goes back for far longer, well over 150 years, back to those Victorian times when travel to Ireland was almost entirely in the hands of fledgling railway companies, whose entrepreneurs invested large sums of money into the building of both ships and harbours. Investment always comes at some risk, and mainly as a consequence of the Great War, in order to stem continuing losses, in 1923 the railways themselves were morphed into the 'Big Four' (Great Western, London Midland Scottish, London North Eastern Railway and Southern Railway)

The aftermath of the Second World War would see a repeat, with the railways and their shipping arms in a very poor state. Nationalisation of the railway system in 1948, seemed to be the only logical answer, the resulting six geographic regions having some independence under the umbrella of the British Transport Commission (BTC). During the early 1950s railway shipping was still in a 1930s mode (passenger, mail and crane loaded cargo), with drive-on ferries almost non-existent. Embryo services did exist at Dover, including its train ferries both there and at Harwich and along with the Atlantic Steam Navigation's routes from Tilbury to Antwerp and Preston to Larne. An unused exception was at Stranraer where a ramp

The ill-fated *Princess Victoria* (1947) which sank in heavy seas in January 1953 following water getting trapped on the vehicle deck. *(Ferry Publications Library)*

had been installed in 1938 in preparation for a vehicle service to Larne using the purpose-built *Princess Victoria* (1939), diesel-driven and way ahead of its time. Sadly, in May 1940, whilst on Admiralty duty she was sunk by an enemy mine off the Humber Estuary. Her 1947 successor of the same name fared little better, sinking in heavy seas in January 1953 after huge waves had damaged her low stern gates allowing water to pour onto the car deck. The freeing ports were totally inadequate, unable to drain it off quickly enough with 113 people losing their lives. It would be another eight years before the ramp was put to good use again.

In 1957, the BTC established a separate Shipping and International Services Division (SISD) to ensure better cohesion and uniformity in the design of ships and in their operational standards. A decade on in 1969, this became known as the British Rail Shipping and International Services Division which, in the following year, adopted the marketing name Sealink. For the most part the new company simply took over the operations of the existing ferries and routes of the former railway operators. The SISD was part of a consortium involved in running ferry services to France, Belgium and the Netherlands in partnership with French National Railways (SNCF), Belgian Maritime Transport Authority (RMT) and the Dutch Zeeland Steamship Company (SMZ) respectively. Collectively, at that time, with 82 ships (not counting tugs and

SCOTLAND

Cairnryan

Larne
(2011)

(1995)

Stranraer

NORTHERN
IRELAND

Belfast

(2014)

Heysham

Fleetwood

Dublin

Dun Laoghaire

(2015)

Holyhead

Birkenhead
(Liverpool)

IRELAND

WALES

ENGLAND

Rosslare

Fishguard

**Stena Line**

2020 routes

Former routes

Cherbourg

FRANCE

Top: The *St Columba* at Fishguard in 1982 in readiness to cover for the *Stena Normandica*'s refit. *(Miles Cowsill)*

Above: The *Earl William* swings off the berth at Cherbourg in July 1985 on her Starliner service to Portsmouth. *(Miles Cowsill)*

Middle right: The *Stena Sea Lynx* departing Rosslare in 1993 on another high- speed dash to Fishguard. *(Miles Cowsill)*

Right: The *Stena Galloway* is viewed departing Belfast with her 1830 service to Stranraer, April 2001. *(John Bryant)*

dredgers) on 19 routes with 11 ports or terminals this partnership became one the most well-known and dominant ferry company operations around Europe.

By the mid-1970s the flow of passengers and freight arriving at ferry ports by rail was showing signs of a decline, as air travel was increasing in popularity along with a boom in car ownership. Ships with full roll on-roll off characteristics were now becoming a pre-requisite and this gave increasing weight to the argument that there was no longer a strong business reason for the ferry services to be owned by the railways. Anticipating this in 1979 the company became Sealink UK Ltd, as a means of preparing it for possible privatisation. On 20th February 1980, the Government made an announcement to that effect and the die was cast.

In 1984 several organisations including Ellermans, Trafalgar House, Common Brothers (Newcastle) and a Sealink Consortium formally expressed an interest. In the event Sea Containers were the only party to submit a bid for Sealink offering £66m for a business estimated to be worth around £170m. It was accepted by the Government and, as a result, Sea Containers inherited no less than 37 ships, 7 harbours (+ 8 quays/piers) together with a workforce of nearly 9,500 of which 2,500 were salaried. Their first act was to rebrand the company as Sealink British Ferries.

James Sherwood, Sea Containers President, was a colourful character, somewhat impulsive, very hands on and used to getting his own way. He loved making decisions, sometimes before they had been discussed by his senior management teams! There was little doubt that he was an astute financier and entrepreneur and his acquisition of Sealink was part of a desire to further diversify his company's portfolio of interests. From the outset, he made it clear that he didn't like negative figures on balance sheets, so if individual port and ship operations failed to make a profit then they ran the risk of being closed down or sold off. From an Irish Sea point of view the Fishguard, Holyhead and Stranraer operations were on safer ground, all showing profits.

The first years were, not surprisingly, characterised by numerous labour disputes, particularly over the manning and working practices on board the ferries. There were also terse discussions with senior colleagues and consortium partners as James Sherwood attempted to get his message across. He made it known that he wanted to shed the image of the old 'Sealink' and this would include phasing out rail passenger activities as soon as practicable seeing the future purely in vehicle ferries, albeit with high quality cruise ship facilities. It was to be a steep learning curve for Sea Containers as they found it difficult to understand the workings of the organisation they had purchased, together with the complexities of unravelling Sealink British Ferries from British Rail.

It did not help that the promises of major new tonnage for Stranraer, Dover and the Channel Islands all failed to materialise, as did the proposed new routes from Dover and Harwich fail to get off the ground. One initiative that did come to fruition was a luxury cruise service from Venice to Istanbul. This was an extension of Sea Containers' London to Venice Simplon Orient Express train service (VSOE) using the ex Silja Line vessel *Silja Star* renamed as *Orient Express*. Still on the negative side, the much vaunted 'Starliner/Sunliner' service to the Channel Islands was an unmitigated financial disaster which led in the end to the company being barred from the Islands. Likewise, wanting a greater share of the receipts from the Dover-Oostende service ended up with their Regie voor Maritiem Transport colleagues getting them shut out of Belgium altogether.

On the plus side there was investment on the Isle of Wight services including the provision of two new fast craft. Progress too was also being made in the internal refurbishment of the fleet, with dedicated motorists' lounges, improved catering outlets and enhanced duty-free shopping facilities. It was only towards the end of Sea Containers' tenure in 1989, with the introduction of two converted freight ships for the Dover-Calais route in the form of the *Fantasia* and her French operated sister *Fiesta,* brought any glimpses of what might be in store when setting new standards in cross-Channel passenger comfort. Similarly, on the Fishguard-Rosslare service the introduction of the Swedish built *Felicity* on long-term charter from  AB Gotland did bring a real touch of class to the Irish Sea.

After an unexpected loss of £12m by SBF in 1984 Sea Containers as a whole reported a profit of around £30m in 1985, which was then followed by a company loss of £36m in 1986, much being blamed on SBF. However, by 1987 SBF was again in profit to the tune of £28m, such was the 'topsy-turvey' world of their fortunes. James Sherwood admitted at that time that a number of strategic mistakes had been made, but felt progress was being made in the shedding the old railway image through new working practices which reduced many of the operational costs, thus auguring well for the future.

So why were Stena Line so keen to want to purchase Sealink British Ferries? It had all begun quietly enough when Stena Ab purchased 8% of Sea Containers shares in March 1989. The company had been looking to expand and had already done so when purchasing the British Columbia Steamships Company in Canada (although this venture failed becoming a victim of vested interests in the USA) and were also bidding for Stoomvaart Maatschappij Zeeland (Zeeland Steamship Company - SMZ) who operated on the Hoek van Holland-Harwich route.

They saw in Sealink British Ferries an opportunity for growth particularly in relation to the strengthening ties within the European Community. Stena believed that their 'Travel Service Concept' would be a good fit and would help increase sales particularly in off-peak sailings. Stena Ab's offer of £259m for the ferry business was accepted by Sea Containers (as was Tiphook's bid of £321m for most of their container enterprises) and included the ports of Fishguard, Holyhead, Stranraer and Harwich Parkeston Quay, all of which Stena felt had the greatest potential. In reality, Stena's acquisition from Sea Containers for Sealink British Ferries was in reality a bit of a mixed bag with an ageing fleet in a rapidly changing world.

Once they had assumed full control in April 1990 Stena Ab, as the parent company, transferred the assets of Sealink British Ferries (SBF) to their subsidiary Stena Line who in turn rebranded it as Sealink Stena Line. In an unsurprising move in November 1992 this trading name was subtly changed to Stena Sealink Line in order to bring more emphasis and authority to the Stena name.

Stena senior staff had visited many ships across the existing fleet during the takeover proceedings but of the 15 ferries they that they acquired only 8 would be considered as having any kind of long-term future with the company. The Irish Sea operations did well out of this as six of them would, within 18 months, become permanent fixtures on the three main routes. They were the long term chartered *Felicity, St Columba* and the four 'saint' class ships named at that time as *Galloway Princess, St Anselm, St Christopher* and *St David* which in due course became the *Stena Galloway, Stena*

*Cambria, Stena Antrim* and *Stena Caledonia* reflecting their route deployment on the Irish Sea. Of the remaining ships only the *Fantasia* at Dover and *St Nicholas* at Harwich were considered as suitable for long term service.

Favourites such as the *Darnia* based at Stranraer, *Earl William* (Liverpool-Dun Laoghaire) and the (*Stena*) *Hengist* and (*Stena*) *Horsa* from Folkestone which regularly covered refits on the Irish Sea were on the 'at risk' list. The latter two were said to be 'homely and comfortable' but at 18 years too small and dated to warrant any new investment. All would be gone by the end of 1992 along with other minor units which included the freight vessels *Cambridge Ferry* and *St Cybi*, considered no longer suitable for further employment.

In addition to the £259m paid for SBF, Stena Line also intended to invest a further £178m to develop their 'Travel Service Concept' initiative aimed at encouraging guests to travel at off-peak times when ships were largely underused. Much of Stena's interior design work was by Figura of Gothenburg who began a programme of upgrading the passenger areas resembling modern shopping malls with improved family-friendly catering options, play areas for children and the revamping of bar lounges to make them suitable for live entertainment. This glitzy open-plan approach was very different to what had gone before. The investment also included bringing in fresh (but not necessarily new) tonnage aimed at improving the East Coast and English Channel operations from Harwich and Dover, respectively. A new route from Southampton to Cherbourg was also created using the *St Nicholas* displaced from the Essex port.

The Irish Sea ships, which were generally in better shape, also received upgrades with the greatest amount of money being spent on the *St Columba* which emerged from her £7m refit at Lloyd Werft, Bremerhaven as the *Stena Hibernia*.

The duty-free boom was beginning to take off in earnest with 'Sail for a Pound' offers promoted through the national newspapers, and as a result passenger numbers escalated and revenue increased. However, the expected profit envisaged by Stena in 1990 was in fact a trading loss and was to be followed by a further pre-tax loss of over £28m by September 1991. The company published 'Operation Benchmark' which set out measures designed to stem and eventually reverse the losses. The upshot was that over a quarter of the 6,000 workforce would lose their jobs, pay would be frozen and all new

Dignitaries and workers at the China Merchants Jinling Shipyard, Weihai, prepare for the naming and float out of the *Stena Estrid* on 16th January 2019. *(CMI Jinling Weihai Shipyard)*

investment curtailed. A third of these job losses (568) would come from the closure of the Folkestone-Boulogne route. Financial experts from within the industry were generally of the opinion that whilst the company had paid too much for SBF the main problem still lay in the high operational and manning costs, an issue the previous owners had in reality failed to properly address. All of this would have repercussions across the whole of the fleet, the Irish Sea operations proving no exception.

The focus of this book is to take a closer look at Stena Line's Irish Sea shipping operations as they found them in 1990 and to celebrate their achievements some 30 years on. It is also important to put this into context as none of today's operations would be there without the those determined entrepreneurs who put their money and faith into such ventures, often amidst strong opposition who chose not to see the benefits of such far-sighted projects.

Today, Stena Line's renowned visionary skills continue to be much in evidence backed by a willingness to invest, as shown when ordering three of the first four E-Flexer series of ferries being constructed in China to grace the waters of the Irish Sea. Two are already in service, the *Stena Estrid* on the Central Corridor's Holyhead-Dublin route and the *Stena Edda* on the Birkenhead -Belfast service and in early 2021 Stena Line will have a third E-Flexer, *Stena Embla,* in service on the latter route.

Of particular interest is how Stena Line have transformed their North Channel services over the last decade with the opening of an impressive new port just north of Cairnryan in 2011. This also included the introduction of two high class ships (*Stena Superfast VII* and *Stena Superfast VIII*) tailored specifically to the route's needs. This £200m major investment involved working with the port authorities at Belfast to further enhance the facilities there for both the Cairnryan and Birkenhead services. When Stena invests it does so with the long-term view in mind. This is in sharp contrast with a world where making profits in the short term is the only aim. Stena's approach is different, it stands out and is far superior. Stena vision indeed!

TWO

# Southern Corridor Fishguard-Rosslare-Cherbourg

### Early Days

Located in the north part of Pembrokeshire the port of Fishguard is in a relatively sheltered bay between Dinas Point in the north and Crincoed Point to the west. Geographically it is only 54 nautical miles across the St George's Channel (which technically separates the Celtic Sea to the south from the Irish Sea to the north) to Ireland.

The construction of Fishguard Harbour was under the aegis of the Fishguard and Rosslare Railways Act of 1899 with the completed Welsh port not opening until 1906, thus making it the youngest of the established 'corridor' routes. The new port and service to Rosslare proved to be a great success. On the other side of the St George's Channel the Great Southern & Western Railway of Ireland (GSWR) did their part by opening a new 37 mile long railway to the port of Rosslare from Waterford. At the port itself, the existing pier was extended and buildings erected in order to accommodate the ships on the new route.

### The Car Ferries Arrive

Fishguard's services to Rosslare didn't change format for many decades and even through to the early 1960s were in the hands of traditional passenger ferries, the *St Andrew* (3,035gt), dating from 1932 and *St David* (3,482gt), a post-war replacement built in 1948. With greater car ownership the demand for crane-loaded car space had increased markedly and so in 1964 British Rail decided to convert the *St David* into a side-loading car ferry. At Fishguard, this was all very well

providing you did not have a medium plus sized vehicle when negotiating the narrow tunnel to the ship, one which had previously been used for herding cattle on and off the boats.

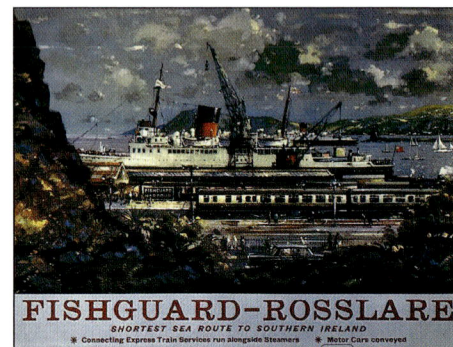

**FISHGUARD—ROSSLARE**
SHORTEST SEA ROUTE TO SOUTHERN IRELAND
✳ Connecting Express Train Services run alongside Steamers    ✳ Motor Cars conveyed

Up to then in summer, in order to free up space, the cargo ship *Slieve Donard* (1960, 1,598gt) would assist, though car owners had to travel by the regular ferry and wait for the cargo ship's arrival. It was worse at Rosslare as at that time there was no road link along the pier only a railway which meant cars had to be crane-loaded on and off flat trucks, a very time-consuming business.

The *St Andrew* finally retired in May 1967 and was replaced by the Heysham

**GREAT WESTERN RAILWAY**
**The Direct Route to IRELAND VIA FISHGUARD**
TO BE OPENED IN SUMMER 1906
MAGNIFICENTLY APPOINTED TURBINE STEAMERS, 22½ KNOTS.

The *St David* (3,482gt) was a replacement passenger ship dating from 1948 for the Fishguard-Rosslare service. This image was taken before British Rail converted her in 1964 into a side-loading car ferry. She was withdrawn in 1970. *(Ferry Publications Library)*

The elegant *Avalon* backing on to her berth at Rosslare; she was converted into a stern loading car ferry in 1975. *(Ferry Publications Library)*

Another vessel converted into a car ferry in 1970 was the *Duke of Lancaster* pictured here at Rosslare. *(Ferry Publications Library)*

A rare image of the *Caledonian Princess* (1961) departing Fishguard in the early 1970s. She saw service on all the Irish Sea routes as well as those to the Channel Islands, before bowing out at Dover in September 1981. *(Ferry Publications Library)*

The *Anderida* (1972) captured arriving at Fishguard, this versatile freight ferry served all of Sealink's four Irish Sea routes in the 1970s. *(Miles Cowsill)*

The *Lord Warden* (1952) was the first car ferry built for British Railways. In 1978 she transferred to Fishguard for a summer service to Dun Laoghaire. *(Ferry Publications Library)*

Observed here at Rosslare, the introduction of the *Stena Normandica* to the Fishguard-Rosslare route in 1979 was a real boost as she was able to carry up to 116 trailers or 470 cars on two full height vehicle decks. *(Miles Cowsill)*

Chartered from 1974 until 1977 for freight services to Rosslare the *Preseli* (ex *Isatal*) approaches the berth at Fishguard. *(Ferry Publications Library)*

steamer *Duke of Rothesay* (4,797gt), which had recently been converted into side-loading car ferry. By 1969 the 'Duke' was joined by the *Caledonian Princess* (3,630gt), from the Stranraer-Larne route which had been built as a stern-loading vehicle ferry (103 cars) from the outset. It wasn't until 1971 however, that a linkspan at Fishguard was actually in place. In 1974 after a substantial refit, the *Duke of Rothesay* was finally given a stern door and so could use the linkspan. The *Caledonian Princess* found it difficult to keep to schedule in bad weather and a succession of other ships including the *Holyhead Ferry I* (1965, 3,879gt) and the freighter *Preseli* (1970, 3,633gt) operated from time to time when the 'Caley P' was not available, usually with mechanical issues. The *Caledonian Princess* made her last crossing on the Fishguard service in June 1975 to be temporarily replaced by another ex-Heysham steamer, the *Duke of Lancaster* until her permanent replacement, the elegant ex-Harwich passenger ferry *Avalon* arrived. The *Avalon* had also been converted into a stern-

17

Top: A contrast in size at Rosslare between the *Princessan Desiree* (B+I Pembroke Dock service) and *Stena Normandica* on the adjacent berth. *(Miles Cowsill)*

Above: A well-laden *St Brendan* (ex *Stena Normandica*) departs Rosslare for Fishguard. *(Miles Cowsill)*

Middle right: Fishguard with the *St David* covering for the *Stena Normandica*'s refit. *(Miles Cowsill)*

Right: The *St Christopher* arriving at Fishguard for the first time having been drafted in whilst on her delivery voyage to Dover in March 1981. *(Miles Cowsill)*

A powerful side view of the *St Columba* accelerating away from Fishguard whilst covering the *Stena Normandica*'s annual refit. *(Miles Cowsill)*

Bow thrusts working hard as the *St David* sets off on another crossing from Fishguard to Rosslare. *(Miles Cowsill)*

loading car ferry and was to prove a great success on the route.

Cutbacks in 1977 on Sealink's Irish services meant a rationalisation on the Fishguard-Rosslare service, the upshot being that in future the *Avalon,* supplemented by the freight ship *Anderida,* would operate just one return service each day. In an unusual move they also brought in the Dover car ferry *Lord Warden* (1952) to start up a summer service in 1978 from Fishguard to Dun Laoghaire but, not unsurprisingly, this was unsuccessful and not repeated in the following year.

## The Big One

Threatened by news of a rival service by B&I from Rosslare to Pembroke Dock, Sealink announced that after berthing trials in September 1978 with sister ship, *Stena Nordica*, that the *Stena Normandica* had been chartered for an initial period of 19 months until the arrival of a new ship currently

Top: **Photographed in the short-lived joint B+I/Sealink livery introduced in 1986, the** *St Brendan* **powers away from Fishguard bound for Rosslare.** *(Miles Cowsill)*

Above: **SNCF's (Sealink Dieppe Ferries)** *Senlac* **at Calais being prepared for her 1986 summer stint on the B+I/Sealink service to Rosslare.** *(Miles Cowsill)*

Middle right: **A striking aerial view of the** *St Brendan* **loading lorries at Fishguard, note the joint livery.** *(Ferry Publications Library)*

Right: **Captured departing Fishguard, in both 1984 and 1985 the Folkestone based ferry** *Hengist*, **covered refits on Rosslare service.** *(Miles Cowsill)*

being built at Belfast. She would be the first diesel-powered passenger/vehicle ferry to serve on the route. Able to load bow and stern she presented a box-like appearance which made her look bigger than she actually was, measuring 5,490gt, with a length of 121m. Her service speed was relatively modest at 17.5 knots but more than adequate for the Fishguard-Rosslare service and able to accommodate up to 1400 passengers in comfortable surroundings. However, it was her massive vehicle carrying capacity for 470 cars or 116 trailers on two full height vehicle decks that really caught the imagination. Advertised locally as the 'Big One' this ship was destined to become a game changer on the Fishguard service.

The *Stena Normandica* had been built by Rickmers Werft, Bremerhaven in 1974 for Stena Line, the first in a series of four very successful ships intended for charter work, her sisters being the *Stena Nautica, Stena (Marine) Atlantica* and *Stena Nordica*. The latter two saw UK service as the *Reine Astrid* for RMT (Oostende-Dover/Ramsgate) and *Sardinia Vera* for Transmanche (Newhaven-Dieppe). Other than the *Reine Astrid,* three remain in active service in the Mediterranean.

Her introduction as from 3rd April 1979 meant only one ship would be needed in the future, the *Avalon* moving north to Holyhead and the *Anderida* returning to Dover. The route had an immediate boost with passenger and freight carryings both increasing by 10%. A side door was fitted to her starboard upper vehicle deck to enable her to load and unload at Fishguard more quickly. On the downside, the *Stena Normandica* encountered several mechanical problems during her early years on the route which, coupled with her scheduled refits, meant that vessels from around the fleet had to cover for her including the *Stena Nordica* which found it difficult to keep to schedule. Other vessels having to cover for her included the *Avalon, St Christopher* (hastily diverted from her delivery voyage to Dover in 1981!), *St Columba* and *St David*, the latter ship being originally earmarked to replace her permanently at Fishguard.

However, the Sealink management were more than happy with her performance and extended her initial charter from Stena Line. After the privatisation of the company and sale to Sea Containers in 1984, early in the following year 1985, she was purchased outright from Stena by their operating division Sealink British Ferries, shortly afterwards being renamed *St Brendan* after a 6th century Irish saint well known for his sea

Seen departing Fishguard, the *Earl Harold* saw employment in both 1987 and 1988 to Rosslare as cover for the *St Brendan. (Miles Cowsill)*

With bow-visor raised, the *Vortigern* cautiously approaches the linkspan at Fishguard whilst on refit cover in January 1987. *(Miles Cowsill)*

A striking aerial publicity view of the *St Brendan* in her new Sealink British Ferries livery dating from 1985.
*(Ferry Publications Library)*

voyages. This came at a time when SBF and B+I Line (British and Irish Steam Packet Company) were in discussions trying to resolve over capacity on the Irish Sea. The latter's Rosslare-Pembroke Dock service was suspended with the loss of 535 jobs, SBF handing all the joint traffic from Fishguard.

The *St Brendan* then encountered a reoccurrence of her mechanical problems which resulted in Folkestone's *Hengist* and later their *Vortigern* being sent to relieve her. In 1986 the *St Brendan* returned from her latest refit with joint Sealink and B+I markings on her hull and funnel, a move which did not go down to with SBF personnel at Fishguard. For the summer months the *Hengist*'s near sister *Senlac*, now under Sealink Dieppe Ferries aegis was employed on the route, displaying a version of the joint service on her hull sides. By the end of the year this joint working arrangement was discontinued and B+I went back to Pembroke Dock.

It was becoming increasingly clear, notwithstanding more mechanical issues in 1988 (covered by the *Darnia* and *Earl Harold*), that the *St Brendan* also needed back up in the summer months to move freight. As a result, both the *Stena Sailor* (later renamed *St Cybi*) as and *Cambridge Ferry* were called up to assist.

The sheer size and capacity of the *Stena Normandica/St Brendan* had taken many by surprise when she first arrived in 1978, but in the ensuing dozen years that followed, she found herself now too small and something bigger was needed. She had been a great favourite with all at Fishguard, with her versatile loading capabilities and from a master's point of view had excellent seagoing qualities and ease of handling, but in her latter years had now begun to look rather tired.

The *St Brendan* would make her last sailing on 11th March 1990 from Rosslare and, after de-storing, was handed over to her new owners, Moby Lines (Italy) who renamed her *Moby Vincent* for their services between Livorno and Bastia.

## A new Jumbo

Rumours of new jumbo ship were rife (TT Linie's *Peter Pan* being a prime contender) but nothing happened until in September 1989 when SBF announced plans to introduce the largest and most luxurious ferry yet to serve on the Irish Sea on a five-year charter. She was the *Visby* built for AB Gotland for their services between Gotland and the ports of

Top left: The *Felicity* is photographed at Dunkerque after her refit at Tilbury, prior to sailing down the English Channel to Rosslare in late February 1990. *(John Hendy)*

Top right: The *Felicity*'s capacious Show Lounge and Bar, aft on Deck 6 *(Miles Cowsill)*

Above: Looking resplendent, the *Felicity* berthed at Rosslare during her first week of service in March 1990. *(Miles Cowsill)*

Middle right: The stylish Tara waiter service restaurant on board the *Felicity* - Deck 7. *(Miles Cowsill)*

Right: The *Felicity* boasted a dedicated deck for cars, caravans and motor homes. *(Miles Cowsill)*

This stunning overhead view of the *Felicity* show her spacious outside deck space, much appreciated by passengers in fine weather. *(Ferry Publications Library)*

The *Stena Cambria* (ex *St Anselm*) arriving at Fishguard, in both 1990 and 1992 she covered the (now) *Stena Felicity*'s refits. *(Miles Cowsill)*

Nynäshamn and Oscarshamn, to the south of Stockholm. Her availability came as a result of AB Gotland losing the franchise for that route to Gotlandslinjen. Built in 1980 and measuring 23,775gt (under the new rules) she was 146m in length with a service speed of 21 knots. She could carry 2,072 passengers, 517 cars and 47 lorries or a mixture of the two.

In the meantime, the *St Brendan* soldiered on supported by the *Cambridge Ferry* in the run up to Christmas. As last hurrah, the Irish Sea decided in January 1990 to unleash three weeks of the worst storms ever encountered in that area. Wind speeds of up to 115mph were recorded, the ship continuing to sail when other ferry services on the Irish Sea were cancelled.

The design brief for the *Visby* had been to create a high capacity ship, which could operate in the restricted waters of her home port, and during the summer months able to undertake high-speed crossings. On entry into service her deadweight proved to be some 800 tonnes more than

An classic image of the *Felicity* at speed during her first season of service on the Irish Sea. *(FotoFlite)*

A contrast in size at Rosslare in the early 1990s; B+I's *Isle of Inishmore* (ex *Leinster*) is dwarfed by the *Stena Felicity*. (Miles Cowsill)

expected increasing her draught to 5.28m, with the depth of water available at Visby only 6.0m! Problems with her cooling system saw her out of action for the rest of that first year, but she settled down to give good service until being released for charter work by her owners in 1989.

The ship's passenger facilities were spread over much of the ship's eleven decks, other than Decks 3, 4 and 5, which were the car decks and Deck 9 being mostly taken up by officers' accommodation. Lowest down in the ship on Deck 2 were 4-berth couchettes, a 200-seater cinema and solarium/sauna health club, whilst higher up on Decks 6, and 7 were a mixture of cabins forward, with the restaurants, bars and shops aft. Deck 8 consisted of cruise cabins and crew accommodation. Deck 10 housed a 448-seater sky lounge, with Deck 11 being a sheltered sun deck.

A £2m refit at Tilbury included refurbishing the bars, shopping areas and restaurants and the fitting of two side loading doors on Deck 5 to provide a high-level access for cars at both Fishguard and Rosslare. The *Felicity*, as she was now named, arrived at Rosslare on 2nd March for berthing trials and followed these up later that day at Fishguard. Commencing her maiden commercial service three days later, on 5th March 1990, the *Felicity* proved to be a very popular ship on the route, not only for passengers who were very impressed with the facilities on offer, but also with freight

27

## Cambridge Ferry at Fishguard

Above: **The ex-Harwich train ferry *Cambridge Ferry* proved to be a useful freight carrier across the Irish Sea, pictured here departing Fishguard in her old Sealink livery.** *(Miles Cowsill)*

Left: **The rail tracks are clearly evident on the *Cambridge Ferry*'s main deck.** *(Miles Cowsill)*

Opposite page

Top left: **A freshly repainted *Cambridge Ferry* eases her way through the lock gates at Milford Haven in 1990.** *(Miles Cowsill)*

Lower left: **The *Cambridge Ferry* in layup at Milford Haven.** (Miles Cowsill)

Top right: **Looking aft from the bridge of the Cambridge Ferry.** *(Miles Cowsill)*

Middle right: **The well-kept and comfortable dining room on board the *Cambridge Ferry*.** *(Miles Cowsill)*

Bottom right: **A memory of bygone times, the beautifully maintained traditional wheelhouse layout on the *Cambridge Ferry*.** *(Miles Cowsill)*

The *Stena Felicity*, seen here departing Fishguard, went through a number of minor livery changes in her time on the Irish Sea, depicted here in her second guise as Sealink Stena Line, previously it was Sealink British Ferries. *(Miles Cowsill)*

The *Stena Lynx* which almost halved the crossing times on the Fishguard-Rosslare route, is seen here manoeuvring to the layby berth at Fishguard, March 1997. *(John Bryant)*

In her fourth and final livery the *Stena Felicity* gets underway from Fishguard in March 1997. *(John Bryant)*

In a third and more subtle livery alteration for the *Stena Felicity*, the company name changed its name in November 1992 to Stena Sealink Line, so as to emphasise the 'Stena' ownership more clearly. *(Miles Cowsill)*

operators who had their own separate accommodation and dining room. Her entry into service came at a time when the Stena Line takeover of Sealink British Ferries was being completed.

## Stena Line takes over

Many knowledgeable observers have commented that the *Felicity* was possibly one of the best investments made on the route up to that time, though some of her early sailings in 1990 were marred by technical issues, one resulted in her being taken out of service and her schedules being covered by the *Horsa* which was currently based at Holyhead. In the autumn, Sealink Stena Line, as they were now known, announced a £4.5m upgrade of the port facilities and infrastructure at Fishguard.

Scheduled refits brought new vessels to the route. Her refit at Falmouth in the late autumn of 1990, was covered by the

*Stena Cambria,* with the ship returning as the *Stena Felicity*. In the weeks leading up to Christmas, the *Cambridge Ferry* was reactivated to lend freight support continuing to do so through the following year as traffic steadily increased. On the 27th December 1990 the *Stena Felicity* carried no less than 516 cars on her afternoon sailing to Rosslare from Fishguard which at the time was a port record. Her 1992 refit was again covered by the *Stena Cambria,* this time she emerged sporting the slightly amended Stena Sealink Line livery. For her January 1994 refit her schedules were covered by Smyril Line's *Norrona.*

1994 was an eventful year on the route which saw the welcome arrival of the *Stena Sea Lynx* fast craft to open a new service from Fishguard to Rosslare. Three sailings a day were initially scheduled for mid-June to mid-July, increasing to no less than five return crossings during the summer peak. Carrying 450 passengers and 90 cars, the 1993 built InCat craft proved a welcome addition on both sides of the Irish Sea

31

Top left: The *Koningin Beatrix* entered service in 1986 for SMZ's Crown Line on the Hoek-Harwich route. *(FotoFlite)*

Top right: A rare image of the *Koningin Beatrix* at Pembroke Dock undertaking berthing trials prior to taking up service at Fishguard in June 1997. *(Miles Cowsill)*

Above: The *Stena Lynx* is about to round the breakwater at Rosslare on her fast craft service from Fishguard. *(Miles Cowsill)*

Middle right: June 22nd 1997 was a wild and wet day forcing the *Stena Felicity* to berth at Pembroke Dock, with Fishguard closed. *(Miles Cowsill)*

Right: Little and large; the first official arrival (3rd July 1997) of the *Koningin Beatrix* at Rosslare, dwarfing the *Stena Lynx*. *(Miles Cowsill)*

The *Condor 10*, pictured approaching Fishguard, was chartered by Stena Line for the summer of 1996 owing to the unavailability of the *Stena Lynx*. *(Miles Cowsill)*

Gareth Cooper, CEO Stena Line UK, Jackie Lawrence, MP for North Pembrokeshire and Captain David Williams head the official party at the transfer of the *Koningin Beatrix* to the UK London register in August 1997. *(Miles Cowsill)*

enabling day excursions to be introduced.

After the disaster in the late September 1993, involving the Baltic ferry *Estonia*, the *Stena Felicity* was one of several Swedish ships to be temporarily withdrawn for checks to their bow doors. The *Stena Sea Lynx* and the chartered freight ship *Vinzia E* covered the scheduled services until her return on 15th October, but restricted to wave heights of less than 4 metres. It wasn't until mid-November she was given the all-clear and the restrictions lifted. In the meantime passengers were scheduled to travel on the *Stena Lynx II* which had transferred from Holyhead, but bad weather put paid to many of the sailings.

By Spring 1995, thought was already being given to a replacement vessel for the *Stena Felicity* as her charter would end in the following year; the *Stena Jutlandica* from the Gothenburg-Frederikshavn route being one of the possible options. Nothing transpired and the search went on with Stena Line able to have her charter extended by a further year. The *Stena Sea Lynx's* summer service continued to attract travellers, being estimated to have carried more than a third of the total number of passengers during that period.

The *Stena Felicity's* 1996 overhaul took her to Germany, her place at Fishguard being taken by the well-travelled *Stena*

*Londoner* (ex *Versailles*). By then all fleet were being rebranded into the new Stena Line corporate livery which meant that in its time on the Irish Sea the *Stena Felicity* had carried the full range of branding from Sealink British Ferries, through to Sealink Stena Line, Stena Sealink Line and finally Stena Line on her hull. With unavailability of the *Stena Sea Lynx* in 1996 Stena chartered in the *Condor 10* fast craft (best known on her services to and from the Channel Islands) which reliably maintained the service.

## The arrival of a Queen

In the Autumn of 1996, Stena Line announced that the *Stena Felicity* would be withdrawn from the route as from 31st March 1997, though in the end it was not until 25th June that she actually did so. With a new fast ferry operation in the form of the HSS *Stena Discovery* starting from Harwich to Hoek van Holland that spring it was clear that one of the two displaced ships, *Stena Europe* or *Koningin Beatrix* could well find themselves on this Irish Sea route. And so it proved, as on 6th November 1996, it being announced the larger of the two ships, the *Koningin Beatrix* would replace the *Stena Felicity*. The route managers were delighted as they were going to

A powerful view of the *Koningin Beatrix* looking at her best in the bright sunshine at Rosslare. *(Miles Cowsill)*

KONINGIN BEATRIX

KONINGIN BEATRIX

Stena Line

receive one of the best-appointed ships in the fleet, which in the summer months, would still have a fast craft operating alongside her.

As a postscript, the *Stena Felicity* returned to its owners Rederi AB Gotland who then carried out a major refit and rebuilding programme before she resumed the name *Visby* once more returning to service with Destination Gotland on the route she was built for. In 2002 she was renamed *Visborg* to free up the name for a new ferry. In 2003 the *Visborg* was sold to Polferries and renamed *Scandinavia* to operate on their Gdansk-Nynasham route over the next twelve years. In 2015, she was purchased by Ventouris Ferries for services between Durres (Albania) and Bari (Italy).

The *Koningin Beatrix* measured 31,910gt, was 162m in length, with a service speed of 21 knots and would be the largest ferry to serve on the Fishguard-Rosslare route, doing so from 1997 until 2002. Built in 1986 the '*KB*', as she was often referred to, had an original capacity for 2,100 passengers with cabin accommodation for 1,296 persons, in practice far too many for the new 3½ hour route. Her garage space was suitably capacious for 550 cars or a mixture of 80 trailers and 275 cars.

She travelled firstly to Rosslare, arriving on 22nd June for berthing trials, the plan being to begin commercial sailings from there three days later. Typically, her debut was greeted by some very unseasonal stormy weather and with fast craft services cancelled and some rival operations stormbound, the *Stena Felicity* continued to operate in order to clear the backlog. From Rosslare, the *Koningin Beatrix* was sent to Pembroke Dock which was more sheltered, for further berthing trials. Needing the aid of two tugs to get her off the berth she undertook a non-scheduled afternoon sailing to Rosslare. She was followed into Pembroke Dock by the *Stena Felicity* (a first time for her), which continued to serve on the crossing to Rosslare until finally finishing with Stena Line on 27th June.

Such were the ferocity of the storms it was not until 3rd July, that the *Koningin Beatrix* was able to make her first official sailing from Fishguard. The following month the ship was registered in London and reflagged to fly the red ensign.

Being so large it was not surprising that the *Koningin Beatrix* needed careful handling in windy conditions, suffering a few berthing mishaps particularly at Rosslare where she had

In December 1998 the larger *Stena Lynx III* successfully took over the fast craft service from Fishguard, trading under the 'Stena Express' banner. Seen here departing Rosslare. *(Miles Cowsill)*

several scrapes and collisions with the port infrastructure. On 7th August 1997, in high winds, the ship was blown on to the lighthouse breakwater at Rosslare, demolishing a part of the quay wall and sustaining damage to her stern and starboard side door. Repairs at Liverpool kept her out of service for five days. On another occasion in 2001 when berthing, a mechanical failure caused the ship's engines to remain stuck in reverse and in the process managed to destroy the adjacent lifeboat pen and badly damage the RNLI's Arun class lifeboat *St Brendan*. Fortunately, no one was hurt.

In 1998 the *Stena Lynx*, as she was now named, returned in April to operate the seasonal fast craft services. The service continued to be such an overwhelming success that from the December 1998 through to September 2011 the route was operated by the larger 81m *Stena Lynx III/Elite* (4,113gt, 37 knots, 660 passengers and 148 cars) trading in a slightly modified livery under the Stena Express banner.

In July 1998 the *Koningin Beatrix* operated in tandem with

In February/March 1999 the ro-pax *Rosebay* from the Harwich-Hoek service covered the *Koningin Beatrix*'s refit; seen here at Fishguard. *(Miles Cowsill)*

the *Stena Challenger* on a charter for the Tour de France to take the support teams and crews, together with TV and media personnel from Cork to Roscoff, the first and only time Stena Line vessels have operated from the port of Cork. A third Stena vessel, *Stena Caledonia*, sailed from Rosslare to Roscoff on the same mission. In all 2,000 passengers and some 4,500m of freight (equivalent to 300 lorries were carried). The P&O freighter *European Pathfinder* from Larne was chartered to move freight during the *Koningin Beatrix's* absence.

For her February 1999 refit the *Koningin Beatrix* was replaced by the *Stena Caledonia* from Stranraer, but she had to return owing to problems with the HSS *Stena Voyager*. The Harwich-Hoek van Holland freighter *Rosebay* (ex *Transgermania*) was called in hastily to move freight. The *Beatrix's* return to Fishguard was further delayed, as at short notice she had to stand in on the Holyhead-Dublin service, not returning to her home port until 17th March.

During 1999 there had been a drop in freight carryings and as a consequence there were the first murmurings of speculation that the *Koningin Beatrix* might be transferred to another route, possibly to the Baltic, where her cabin capacity would be better utilised. A number of contenders were rumoured including the *Prins Filip/Stena Royal* (currently the *Calais Seaways* for DFDS), *Stena Jutlandica* and *Stena Danica* as well as a possible sale of the *Koningin Beatrix* to Brittany Ferries. During her early February 2000 refit her replacement at Fishguard was the ex-Dover ferry *Stena Invicta* which was extended through to mid-March as the *Koningin Beatrix* was also required to stand in on the Holyhead-Dublin service for the *Stena Challenger's* refit.

The fast ferry service which had been such a success continued, but the 2000 season was reduced in length as part of a cost-cutting programme. Figures overall for January-September showed carryings of 721,000 passengers (697,000 in 1999) and 164,000 cars.

At the height of the 2001 summer season the '*Beatrix*' was beset with more mechanical problems meaning that she had to operate at a slower speed. She was withdrawn in early September and sent to Brest for an extensive mechanical overhaul. During her repairs at the Breton port, high winds blew her off the quay and she sustained further damage, not returning to service until the end of October as a result. Her

On Yer Bike?! The *Koningin Beatrix* and *Stena Challenger* berthed at Cork in readiness to transport the Tour de France entourage to Roscoff in July 1998. *(Ferry Publications Library)*

place on the route was covered by the *Stena Galloway* from Stranraer. Soon afterwards it was announced that as from March 2002, in a reciprocal move, the *Koningin Beatrix* and would be transferred to Stena Line's Karlskrona-Gdynia service and be renamed *Stena Baltica* with the *Stena Europe* coming to Fishguard. The *Koningin Beatrix* finished her time on the route on 12th March 2002 and on the following day before sailing to the Baltic she was renamed *Stena Baltica*, entering service on the Karlskrona-Gydnia route on 21st March.

Completing her story, in 2005 she underwent an extensive £20m rebuild at the Remontowa shipyard in Gdansk. This make-over included the refurbishment of the passenger facilities on Decks 7, 8 and 9 together with the creation of a new vehicle deck by removing the cabin accommodation on Decks 5 and 6. This doubled her garage space to 1,800 lane meters allowing 100 lorries to be carried, whilst externally, a large vehicle door and ramp was constructed at the to facilitate double-deck loading.

In June 2011, the *Stena Baltica* was replaced by the *Stena Spirit* and was laid up at Lyeskil, Sweden awaiting sale/charter or further use in the Stena Line fleet. It wasn't until January 2013 that she was reactivated having been purchased by Società Navigazione Alta Velocità (SNAV) and renamed *SNAV*

Photographed arriving at Rosslare, the *Stena Europe* (1981) is the oldest ship in the Stena Line fleet. However, after a 'life extension' rebuild and refurbishment in 2019 she is expected to remain in service for some considerable time. *(Gordon Hislip)*

*Adriatico* for services between Ancona and Split. Since then, she has seen charter work for Ferry Express Panama and Acciona Trasmediterránea between Barcelona and Mahon and today operates for Grandi Navi Veloci (GNV) on their Naples-Palermo service.

### The Stena Europe arrives

The 1981 built *Stena Europe* was smaller (24,828gt, 149m length, 20.5 knots) and older than the *Koningin Beatrix* and whilst this raised a few eyebrows, there was no doubt that she would be a more economic ship to operate. Her original passenger certificate was for 2,076 and at the time had garage space for 470 cars or 60 lorries.

She was built as the *Kronprinsessan Victoria* for Sessan Line and was a sister ship to the *Prinsessan Birgitta* which became the *St Nicholas* at Harwich and *Stena Normandy* at Southampton. Whilst undergoing her sea trials Stena Line

An attractive image of the *Stena Europe* discharging vehicles using the original ro-ro berth at Rosslare. *(Matt Davies)*

bought a majority share in the company which became known as Stena Sessan Line. Initially she served on the Gothenburg-Frederikshavn route before, in 1982, being reconfigured to make her suited as a night ferry on the Gothenburg-Keil service.

In 1989, she was renamed *Stena Saga* and transferred to the Frederikshavn-Oslo service. By 1994 she was on the move again, this time in a swop of vessels to serve on the Hoek van Holland-Harwich route joining up with the *Koningin Beatrix* and at the same time receiving her current name of *Stena Europe*. As the Harwich-Hook of Holland service didn't require as many cabins but was a busier route for freight, the decision was taken to remove the additional cabin block which had been added to her top deck in a previous rebuild, reducing not only the ship's tonnage but allowing more freight to be carried.

The *Stena Europe* was a successful ship on the Harwich route and continued there until the arrival of the new HSS S*tena Discovery* in 1997. Stena then reallocated her to their Lion Ferry subsidiary between Karlskrona (Southern Sweden) and Gdynia (Poland) renaming her as *Lion Europe,* though within six months Stena Line had fully absorbed the Lion Ferry brand, so she became *Stena Europe* once more.

With the Karlskrona-Gdynia route continuing to grow, in 2002 it was decided to swap the *Stena Europe* with her former Harwich to Hook of Holland running mate *Koningin Beatrix* which would be rebuilt into the *Stena Baltica*. To make her more suitable for the shorter Fishguard to Rosslare route, the *Stena Europe* was sent to Cityvarvet Gothenburg, for conversion back to a day ferry. In addition to upgrading the passenger areas the main thrust of this £4m refurbishment was to increase once more her freight capacity by stripping out the cabins on Deck 5 (the old upper vehicle deck) thus bringing her freight carrying ability up to 100 units. Freight drivers would now enjoy single berth cabins, a segregated restaurant offering both waiter and self-service and their own dedicated lounge with all modern entertainment facilities.

Her arrival at Fishguard was initially greeted with mixed views, how could a 21-year-old ship be an improvement? However, many were pleasantly surprised and the improved facilities for passengers were much appreciated. These included the provision of the Stena Business and Stena Plus Lounges and the eating facilities (even though waiter service had been discontinued owing to low demand) offered plenty

The *Stena Lynx III* arriving off Rosslare, note the Welsh red dragon on her prow and the Stena Express hull branding. *(Gordon Hislip)*

Although viewed here at Dublin, the *Stena Nordica* (2000) has seen much relief service on the Southern Corridor and to Cherbourg. *(Gordon Hislip)*

of variety in a very relaxed environment. The *Stena Europe* soon settled down with the *Stena Lynx III* in the summer months operating in tandem with the conventional ferry.

On 31st January 2003, the *Stena Europe* was hitting the national headlines when in high winds she suddenly lost power en-route from Rosslare. The ferry drifted to within a

This night shot at Holyhead dates from September 2011 after the *Stena Lynx III* had been withdrawn from service. She was almost immediately purchased by South Korean interests. *(Gordon Hislip)*

In March 2019 the *Stena Europe* underwent a major 'life extension' overhaul at the Gemak Shipyard in Tuzla, Turkey. *(Stena Line)*

mile of the Tusker Rock lighthouse and passengers were being prepared to be airlifted off the ship. Fortunately, after an interminable hour, two of her engines were restarted enabling her to make her way slowly to Pembroke Dock which was the

more sheltered and, in this case, a safer harbour.

In 2004, with no suitable replacement available to cover the *Stena Europe's* refit, the route was closed between 31st January and 14th February. However, in 2005 by delaying her refit until May this enabled the *Stena Caledonia* to cover. For 2006, the freighter *Stena Seafarer*, with its limited accommodation, from the Fleetwood-Larne service was able to deputise in the January.

The ensuing years followed a relatively quiet pattern with the fast craft *Stena Lynx III* now owned by Stena Line and marketed under the Stena Express banner. Figures for 2004 showed that the route was now back in profit largely as a result of increases in freight traffic and through the economies made with the introduction of the *Stena Europe*.

The centenary of the route was celebrated in style during August 2006, events included an exhibition at Fishguard Library reflecting the town's maritime history; the arrival of Castle class steam locomotive Earl Bathurst at Fishguard Harbour Station; the launch of the 1906-2006 anniversary book, 'Fishguard-Rosslare' by Miles Cowsill and a three day 'Dolphinathon' aboard the *Stena Europe* monitoring dolphin numbers between Fishguard and Rosslare. Later on came an official visit from Wales' then First Minister, Rhodri Morgan, who paid tribute to the important role the route has played in developing trade and tourism to the area. In Ireland, Rosslare also arranged a series of events to commemorate the bridge between the two ports.

The winter refit programme continued smoothly over the following years with *Stena Nordica* and *Stena Seafarer* often standing in, though when it was only a short refit no cover would be put in place. The summer Stena Express service, now based overnight at Rosslare, continued to carry good loadings though from 2006 it was reduced to two round trips each day. Sadly, the service did not reappear the 2012 season and the *Stena Lynx III* was sold.

Severe weather conditions in October 2012 caused disruption to services, especially at Rosslare. On the 27th of that month with 464 passengers on board the *Stena Europe* was caught by the wind as she attempted to berth, her port bow striking the starboard bow of the Irish Ferries' ship *Oscar Wilde* which was at the adjacent berth. It was several hours before the *Stena Europe* was able to berth, causing the evening sailing to Fishguard to be cancelled.

An graphic image capturing the glow of the early morning light as the *Stena Europe* gently backs towards her berth at Rosslare. *(Gordon Hislip)*

In November 2013, the *Stena Europe* covered the refit of the Holyhead-Dublin ferry *Stena Nordica*, the latter then coming to Fishguard to cover the *Europe's* refit at Cammell Laird's, Birkenhead.

More weather issues on 20th November 2016 saw her caught up in Storm Angus and not able to dock at Fishguard, so she sought shelter off the Llyn Peninsular eventually docking nearly 24 hours later than scheduled.

In January 2017 at Harland and Wolff, Belfast the *Stena Europe* became the first of Stena's Irish Sea fleet to refit and emerged sporting Stena's new strapline 'Connecting Europe for a Sustainable Future' emblazoned on either side of the vessel, reflecting the company's commitment to the environment. The ship was now 36 years old and with work undertaken on her bow thrusters, rudders, main shaft seals as well as increasing the upper vehicle deck height to 4.85m by removing a fixed car deck, let alone upgrades to the galley and crew accommodation, this was seen as an indicator that the ship was likely to remain in service on the Fishguard-Rosslare route for some time yet. The linkspan at Fishguard, which dates from 1972, is still a contentious issue with no replacement in sight after Stena Line in 2018 shelved their original proposals. Its narrow ramp does restrict larger vessels from using the berth especially if they are stern loading.

In early April timetable revisions were put in place, increasing the number of day-time crossings as well as speeding them up by 30 minutes to 3 hours 15 minutes with the overnight crossing from Fishguard extended to 4 hours 15 minutes to facilitate a greater rest period for hauliers.

Traffic figures for 2001 through to 2017 showed a significant decrease in numbers by some 41% from 687,000 in 2001 to 303,249 in 2017. Whilst some of this is attributable to the loss of the fast craft services after 2011 and competition from other ferry operations, there has been a massive change in people's travel habits, in particular being attracted to the budget airlines operating to and from Ireland. However, freight carryings were holding firm and continued to buck the trend.

Confirming that the *Stena Europe* would continue in service beyond her 40th birthday in 2021, Stena Line sent her to the Gemak Shipyard in Tuzla, Turkey in March 2019, for '. Stena Line have an excellent reputation for the longevity of their ships as a result of careful planned maintenance and regular upgrading, for example the *Stena Danica* (1983) on their Gothenburg-Frederikshavn service, so this was not

Built in 2006 as the *Cartour Beta*, the vessel was chartered to Celtic Link Ferries in 2011 as their *Celtic Horizon* for the Rosslare-Cherbourg service. Observed in 2012 at Cherbourg with Brittany Ferries' *Cotentin* in the background. (*Gordon Hislip*)

necessarily a surprise. The expectation was that the *Stena Europe* would return to service on Wednesday 26th June. In the meantime, the *Stena Nordica* was slated to cover her services from Fishguard to Rosslare.

The work being undertaken was understood to be mostly technical with limited changes to the passenger accommodation. Part of the work was to make modifications to the deckhead on the main vehicle deck (Deck 3) allowing full-height trailers to be carried across the entire deck rather than just on the port side.

External works included the renewal of the majority of the ship's windows, the removal of the davit launches from the side promenades to be replaced by Marine Evacuation Systems (MES) and new handrails on the outside deck. In addition, the whole hull would be shot blasted to remove all the existing old paint work in order to improve fuel efficiency and the ship's appearance. Internally, the passenger stairwells were to be revamped, the Barista Coffee outlet redesigned, the Information Desk upgraded and the general décor

throughout the ship improved. Down below, the engines would all undergo a thorough overhaul.

Owing to technical issues, including waiting for specialist parts, there were severe delays to the *Stena Europe's* return on the Fishguard-Rosslare service. The ship finally left Tuzla on 7th September, arriving at Liverpool's Gladstone Dock some eight days later where further work was undertaken. Finally, the ship re-entered service from Rosslare on 22nd September almost three months later than planned and the *Stena Nordica* was able to stand down. Now capable of carrying up to 100 freight units and still with a healthy passenger capacity for 1,400 persons, hopefully the route will fully repay Stena Line's continued investment in this well-loved ferry.

## On the Horizon

On 26th February 2014, Stena Line announced that they had acquired Celtic Link Ferries which had operated from Rosslare to Cherbourg since 2005 with effect from 31st March.

In 2016 Stena Line bought out Celtic Link Ferries including the charter of the *Celtic Horizon*, immediately renaming her *Stena Horizon*. *(Gordon Hislip)*

The full Stena Line livery was applied to the *Stena Horizon* in 2018, she is photographed arriving at Cherbourg in May 2019. *(John Bryant)*

This included their Visentini ro-pax ship *Celtic Horizon* (ex *Cartour Beta*) which dated from 2006 and had been on a five-year charter from the Italian company since 2011, Stena Line subsequently renewing it in 2016. The vessel was immediately renamed *Stena Horizon* and the process of repainting her funnel in the Stena house colours began in Rosslare that same day. She normally operates three crossing each week, departing Rosslare on Tuesdays, Thursdays and Saturdays with returns from Cherbourg on each of the following days.

The route was first established in 1998 by P&O Irish Ferries, the service ceasing as a result of a rationalisation by the parent company in 2004. Early in the following year the route was reactivated by Celtic Link Ferries who saw it as an important export link for livestock and fish to France. With the backing of local investors, it was set up by the Wexford based O'Flaherty and O'Leary families whose local interests include haulage operator O'Leary International, a fish processing plant and the Saltees Fish trawler fleet.

43

As a finale to her service with Stena Line, the *Stena Superfast X* covered refits on most of the Irish Sea routes, including the Rosslare-Cherbourg service in January 2020 where she is viewed at the Irish Port. *(Gordon Hislip)*

The acquisition of the Rosslare-Cherbourg route represented a key strategic investment for Stena Line seeing an opportunity for positive long-term growth in tourist and freight traffic to and from the Continent. Stena's acquisition came at a time when the Irish economy was strengthening.

A near sister of the *Stena Mersey* and *Stena Lagan (*see Chapter 5*)*, she measures 26,500gt, is 186m in length and has a service speed of 23 knots. Her passenger certificate for 750 persons (reduced to 660 for 'passenger comfort') and her vehicle decks can accommodate up to 160 cars and 135 lorries. Whilst she retains much of her Studio Ancora designed interior, Stena has reupholstered much of the seating, including the aft lounge. The company have also introduced their own branding throughout the ship, including Cafe Barista, Met Bar and Stena Shopping. Whilst some of these changes are modest, they have improved the ambience within, the ship now looking far less spartan.

Advertised in Ireland 'as the easy way to Europe' the *Stena Horizon* has been a welcome and reliable addition to the Stena fleet, the route becoming increasingly popular with truckers, car owners and foot passengers. Both unaccompanied and accompanied freight is carried including

a large trade in fresh fish exports to France and Spain. Livestock too is carried with up to 15 or 20 trucks carried per crossing during the height of the calve season. In addition, trade cars are imported for French vehicle manufacturers. The passenger market is equally diverse and includes large numbers of foot passengers, student group coach parties, cars, camper vans as well as motorcyclists.

The versatility of this Visentini class ship has been put to good use and she has been used for refit cover each year serving on the Holyhead-Belfast and Birkenhead-Belfast routes.

For her own February 2016 refit at Harland and Wolff, Belfast  (her Rosslare-Cherbourg service being covered by near sister *Stena Flavia*), the toilets and children's area were refurbished and flooring replaced, together with two cabins being upgraded to 'Captain's Class'. In 2018, after continuing to operate with an unbranded white hull, she emerged from her annual refit wearing the new Stena 'Green Wave' livery, as a result she looked so much better. Her 2019 refit saw her place being taken by the *Stena Nordica* on the Cherbourg service, whilst in 2020 it was the turn of the *Stena Superfast X*.

# THREE

# Central Corridor Holyhead/Liverpool - Dun Laoghaire/Dublin

## Irish Mail

Whilst Holyhead on Anglesey, North Wales, has long been the most important link between London and Ireland with only 57 nautical miles of the Irish Sea to cross, up to 1842 the main route was via Liverpool to Dublin on which the Admiralty mail was carried. Up to that time, as a result, port development at Holyhead was extremely slow with travellers having to use wherries to get on board the sailing ships.

The long-awaited construction and opening of Thomas Telford's bridge in 1826 across the Menai Strait linking Anglesey to the mainland had been a welcome move in the right direction. However, it wasn't until 1844 that Parliament gave approval to the (C&HR) to construct a railway line between the two which would include a bridge over the Menai Strait. In a separate move plans were drawn up to enclose more than 400 acres of deep water at Holyhead in order to create a sheltered roadstead. This included the building of a promenade breakwater 1¾ miles long, the longest in the United Kingdom, taking 28 years to complete. Since then Holyhead has never looked back.

Moving on to more modern times, following the nationalisation of Britain's railways in January 1948 came the introduction of two motorships, *Hibernia* and *Cambria* respectively, replacing their predecessors as the principal passenger mailboats on the Holyhead-Dun Laoghaire service. These two-class vessels, described as being the fastest and

HOLYHEAD
for
DUBLIN AND THE REPUBLIC OF IRELAND
Overnight in comfort by the modern motor ships 'Cambria' and 'Hibernia'—both fitted with anti-roll stabilisers
EVERY NIGHT (ALSO BY DAY IN SUMMER)
BRITISH RAILWAYS

The post-war mailboat *Cambria* at Dun Laoghaire in 1969, her basic schedule called for just one nightly sailing in each direction. *(John Byrne)*

The *Hibernia* (1949) had accommodation for 2,361 passengers. Viewed at Dun Laoghaire in 1975 towards the end of her career. *(Allan Ryszka-Onions)*

largest cross-channel motorships yet, each measured 4,972gt and had accommodation for 2,361 passengers.

Their schedules were, in comparison with today's intensive operations, extremely leisurely with just one nightly sailing in

each direction throughout the year. During their 1964/65 refits both vessels, now 15 years old, underwent a major modernisation programme at their builders Harland and Wolff, Belfast, with lounges reconfigured and old post war-style furnishings removed. Now branded as British Rail, a new corporate image for the ships emerged from the upgrade with red funnels carrying the double arrow logo and hulls painted in monastral blue. 'Times were certainly 'a changing'.

## Entering the Car Ferry Age

Just a year later in 1965, as a response to the growing demands from passengers to take their cars with them. the Holyhead-Dun Laoghaire route received its first car ferry, rather unimaginatively named *Holyhead Ferry I*. The 3,879gt vessel, which had been built by Hawthorn Leslie (Shipbuilders) Ltd on Tyneside at a cost of some £1.6m would be one class only, accommodating 1,000 passengers with garage space for 160 cars. At Holyhead a new berth with a linkspan had been constructed at the Salt Island Admiralty Pier, whilst at Dun Laoghaire a temporary berth on the East Pier was put in place until a more permanent solution could be agreed.

What surprised the more knowledgeable onlookers was that the ship had no drive-through capability, was still powered by steam turbine machinery and lacked direct control of the engines from the bridge save by electric telegraph. Compared to the Scandinavian built ships of this period the *Holyhead Ferry I* was totally outmoded.

Despite entering service some 10 days later than planned (*Normannia* from the Dover-Boulogne route deputising), on 19th July she made her first crossing from Holyhead to Dun Laoghaire. She soon proved to be very popular and her one round trip per day schedule being increased to two on Fridays and Saturdays during the summer peak. During the off season over the next three years she would cover the refits of the Stranraer car ferries, whilst in 1968/9 she substituted for the *Hibernia* which was standing in on the Harwich-Hoek van Holland service.

By 1969 the growth of vehicle traffic on the Holyhead route had not only seen the *Holyhead Ferry 1's* season extended but now called for two ships to operate the service, initially the *Caledonian Princess,* before near sister *Dover* was able to be released from her home port. At Dun Laoghaire in the March

Launch day at Hawthorn Leslie (Shipbuilders) Ltd, Tyneside, 17th February 1965, for the rather unimaginatively named *Holyhead Ferry I*. The £1.6m, 3,879gt car ferry, had accommodation for 1,000 passengers and 160 cars. *(Ferry Publications Library)*

In 1970 Freightliner Terminals were opened at Holyhead, Dublin and Belfast, serviced by two new container ships, *Brian Boroime* (seen here) and *Rhodri Mawr*. Both had the dubious reputation of being able to 'roll on wet grass'. *(Mike Griffiths)*

the new St Michael's Wharf car ferry terminal was opened, with linkspans on either side of the pier. This gave greater flexibility and was extremely useful in enabling ships to berth on the sheltered side of the pier during inclement weather.

In May 1971, the Britannia Tubular Bridge was seriously damaged by a fire, caused by two boys searching for bird nests and using lighted newspapers as torches, severing the rail link to the mainland. The lining of the bridge was formed with old railway sleepers covered in creosote and so was highly flammable. Consequently, the mail boat and rail connected cargo services were switched to operate from Heysham to Dun Laoghaire, adding another 4 hours to the crossing times. During mid-June British Rail chartered the heavy load carrier *Kingsnorth Fisher* to retrieve some eleven diesel locomotives trapped at the Anglesey port. On the 30th January 1972, the bridge was reopened and amidst much celebration the mail boats resumed their service to and from Holyhead to Dun Laoghaire.

The cargo/cattle vessel *Slieve Donard* (1959) had a stern door allowing 60 cars to be carried on peak back-up services. *(Author's Collection)*

In the meantime, cargo operations had been moving towards full containerisation with new Freightliner Terminals at Holyhead, Dublin and Belfast. In 1970 two new container ships, *Brian Boroime* and *Rhodri Mawr* (4,098gt), arrived to

The *Holyhead Ferry I* is pictured at the Carlisle Mailboat Pier, Dun Laoghaire on a layover, with astern, the Waveney Class RNLI Lifeboat 44-006. *Arthur and Blanche Harris.* (*Ferry Publications Library*)

The ex-Heysham steamer *Duke of Lancaster* at Dun Laoghaire on her summer services to Holyhead in the late 1970s. (*John Hendy*)

serve these three ports, traffic growing rapidly and carrying over 70,000 containers in 1973. The arrival of these ships and of the vehicle ferries saw the rapid demise of the old traditional cargo/cattle ships, the last of these, *Slieve Donard* (1960) going out of service in 1975. The container ships remained in service on the routes until 1989, both having the reputation of being able to 'roll on wet grass'.

The *Holyhead Ferry I* remained as principal car ferry to Dun Laoghaire, with the ex-Heysham steamer *Duke of Rothesay* acting as the second vessel, sometimes covering for the *Caledonian Princess* at Fishguard during her winter overhauls. However, in a portent of things to come, between June 1974 and December 1975 she was based at Dover in a reciprocal swap with her near sister *Dover* which offered the greater vehicle capacity (160/205 cars respectively). In 1976 the *Holyhead Ferry I* was sent to Swan Hunter's shipyard on Tyneside for conversion to a drive-through ferry, and renamed *Earl Leofric.* Her vehicle capacity increased to 205 cars, but as

Top: All flags flying the *St Columba* arrives at Holyhead for the very first time on 5th April 1977. *(Ferry Publications Library)*

Above: The 5th August 1981 was a proud day too for the *St David* with her maiden arrival at Holyhead. *(Ferry Publications Library)*

Middle right: The *Earl Siward* (ex *Dover* 1965) regularly served from Holyhead until 1981, seen in early June her last year for Sealink. *(Johan Inpijn)*

Right: A late 1970's view of ro-ro freighter *Dalriada* departing Dun Laoghaire for Holyhead. *(Miles Cowsill)*

a consequence her passenger numbers were reduced to 725. Save for one or two diversions covering refits she remained on the short sea services until being withdrawn in 1981. Sent for scrapping it was an almost inevitable short life for a ship that was basically outdated from the start.

Back in 1974 British Rail announced plans to build a new linkspan at Holyhead's inner harbour and in early 1975 they placed an order with the Aalborg Verft, Denmark for a new passenger/vehicle designed to serve on the Holyhead-Dun Laoghaire route. The traditional mail boats *Hibernia* and *Cambria* would then be withdrawn once the new ship came into service. In the meantime, the *Dover* maintained the car ferry service backed up by the ex-Heysham/Fishguard vessel *Duke of Lancaster* during the summer months.

The new ship was named *St Columba* in honour of the Irish saint and entered service at Holyhead on 27th April 1977. By far the largest ship so far to serve on the Dun Laoghaire crossing, she measured 7,836gt, was 129m in length and had a service speed of 19.5 knots. The *St Columba* had a passenger capacity of 1,600 (augmented to 2,400 in peak times), with garage space for 335 cars or 36 lorries or a mixture of the two. She was an instant success carrying over 1m passengers in her first year. With the boom showing no sign of diminishing over the next few years a variety of ro-ro vessels were used (including, *Dalriada*, *Anderida* and *Stena Timer*) to support the movement of freight.

Whilst the new vehicle ferry berth in the inner harbour made life easier from the operational management and travelling public's viewpoints, for masters of the *St Columba* manoeuvring her out of the confines of the narrow harbour during strong southerly gales could call for nerves of steel. Many ideas were tried depending on the state of the tide and wind direction. One favoured method was to swing by using the piles on the container berth to hold the stern and so be able to exit bow first. An alternative was having warned other shipping beforehand to ensure that their own berthing ropes were secure, on clearing the berth immediately go full astern at breakneck speed until the ship could safely swing outside the Mail Pier dolphin.

On those occasions when the *St Columba* was away on refit or suddenly had to go off-service with mechanical issues there was always great deal of scrabbling around for a suitable replacement. Whilst freighters tended to be more readily

The *St Christopher*, diverted on her delivery voyage to Dover, approaches Holyhead to cover for the *St Columba* on 15th March 1981. *(Ferry Publications Library)*

available, passenger/car ferries were not. Stranraer's *Ailsa Princess* and *Antrim Princess* and Sessan Line's *Princessan Desiree* were all called up to support the *Lord Warden* and *Avalon*, both latter ships ceasing Sealink service in 1979. The *Lord Warden* was sold for pilgrim use out of Jedda, whilst the *Avalon* went to the breakers, a mere 17 years old. Steamships it seemed had now had their day, well almost. For in 1981 the *Dover* (now the drive-through vessel *Earl Siward*) returned to Holyhead for one last hurrah to support the *St Columba's* summer season. She was then sold to Cypriot interests as the *Sol Express* before returning to UK waters in 1993 as a night club venue on the Tyne at Gateshead. The *Tuxedo Royal,* as she was now named, remained there for six years before moving to Middlesborough for a similar venture. This failed dismally and she lay there unloved and unwanted opposite the new Riverside Football Stadium. In 2017, the *Tuxedo Royale* was badly damaged by fire but it wasn't until September 2019 that, having been re-floated (and following asbestos removal ) the ship was towed to  for scrapping.

Earlier in March 1981 with the *St Columba* off service, the brand new Sealink Dover-Calais ferry *St Christopher* was hastily diverted on her delivery voyage from Belfast to cover on the Holyhead-Dun Laoghaire service for 4 days. She created a big impression before continuing to Fishguard for a three-week stint there. Those at Dover were not amused!

51

An attractive image of the *St David* (1981), the last of the 'Saint' class, getting underway at Fishguard bound for Holyhead after covering at the Pembrokeshire port. *(Miles Cowsill)*

The long-awaited arrival of the fourth of the 'Saint' class vessels, *St David*, on 10th August 1981 was a real boost for the route and, as the more economic unit, displaced the *St Columba* on the winter schedules. As with her near sisters her internal ramp arrangements meant that she could operate at any port whether they had a single or double-deck loading.

On 5th March 1982, the rival ferry company B+I was looking to start up a Dublin-Holyhead service in order to make better utilisation of their ships. Sealink employees at Holyhead were totally opposed to this and fearful for their jobs blockaded the entrance to the harbour. In retaliation, a B+I crew boarded their laid-up ferry *Munster* at Dublin and sailed it the few miles along the coast blockading the harbour at Dun Laoghaire. When the *St David* arrived off Dun Laoghaire, she was prevented from entering and after a few attempts and cat and mouse tactics she went back to Holyhead. Returning the next morning they found the *Munster* still blocking the entrance but because there was a sick passenger on board the

Sealink's Holyhead freight vessel *St Cybi* (ex *Stena Sailor*, ex *Dundalk*) closes in on her home port. *(Gordon Hislip)*

*St Columba*, in Sealink British Ferries livery, loading at Dun Laoghaire with, in the background, the *Earl William* having arrived from Liverpool. *(Ferry Publications Library)*

*St David,* following a doctor's call for urgent medical treatment the *Munster* moved aside on humanitarian grounds so that the ship could dock. Following a quick turn round the *St David* sailed once more for Holyhead with all sailings suspended. The issue was finally resolved early in the following month in favour of B+I, thus forming the basis of the ferry operations at Holyhead we see today. Despite the fears that this move would jeopardise jobs, the opposite became true, as increased volumes of traffic opened new opportunities. During her October 1982 refit the *St Columba* became a one class ship, bringing her in line with the rest of the Irish Sea fleet, the *Ailsa Princess* deputising for her in the meantime. In August 1983 with the *St Columba* having another of her mechanical aberrations, the *Villandry* from SNCF was hastily called in to deputise.

With privatisation looming in 1984 the Sealink fleet

gradually lost their British Rail double arrow logo from their funnels. James Sherwood's Sea Containers company were the successful bidder, with Sealink now being marketed as Sealink British Ferries (SBF). On the Central Corridor came promises of fresh investment which included new and larger ferries for Holyhead. However, by early February of the following year SBF and B+I were in discussion aimed at reducing over capacity on the Irish Sea with the *St Columba* operating alongside B+I's *Leinster* and *Connacht.* Industrial disputes within the latter company forced SBF to modify their plans, the *St David* standing in whilst the *St Columba* underwent a major five-week refit in Bremerhaven. In 1987, with traffic building once more, the *Stena Sailor* and Folkestone's *Vortigern* provided extra freight capacity on the Dun Laoghaire service, whilst in 1988 it was the turn of the totally unsuited *Seafreight Highway.* In 1989 the ex-Dover train ferry, *Saint*

53

A magnificent aerial view of Holyhead in the late 1980's with the *St Columba* arriving from Dun Laoghaire, the *Vortigern* in the dry dock and the Freightliner Container Terminal behind. *(Ferry Publications Library)*

During 1990 the *Horsa* became the second ship on the Dun Laoghaire service, photographed at the Irish port as she turns to head for Holyhead. *(Miles Cowsill)*

*Eloi*, covered the *Columba's* refit, arriving at Holyhead in a very uncared for condition which led to many complaints.

The steady growth of ro-ro traffic on the Irish Sea had over the past few years adversely affected carryings on the Freightliner service from Holyhead to Dublin and Belfast, and as a result in 1989 the operation was closed and the two container ships, *Brian Boroime* and *Rhodri Mawr* disposed of. With B+I withdrawing from their Liverpool-Dublin service and concentrating everything on the Holyhead route, SBF saw an opportunity to start up their own service from Liverpool to Dun Laoghaire using their 1964 veteran *Earl William*. After an encouraging start in 1988, mechanical issues and falling patronage saw the route closed on 9th January 1990.

That same month, late morning on 31st January 1990, in gale force winds with 199 passengers on board, the *St Columba* was en-route from Dun Laoghaire and approaching South Stack when a serious fire occurred in the port engine. She was still some 10 nautical miles sailing distance to Holyhead but was forced to drop anchor. Acting quickly, the fuel supply was shut off and both engines stopped. As a precaution a mayday was issued, fortunately the fire was brought under control within 20 minutes and extinguished 10 minutes later. The cause was a design fault resulting in a fractured fuel line. Firemen from Gywnedd were airlifted to the ship by helicopters from 22 Squadron, RAF Valley, to help in the mopping up operations. The ship was towed slowly to Holyhead before going on to Liverpool for repairs. Both the

The *St Columba* was renamed *Stena Hibernia* in March 1991 after her £6m upgrade at Bremerhaven, designed to bring her into line with Stena's much vaunted 'Travel Service Concept'. Here she cautiously approaches the inner harbour at Holyhead. *(Miles Cowsill)*

The superbly fitted out Hibernia Restaurant on board the *Stena Hibernia*, designed to give a feeling of greater space. *(Miles Cowsill)*

The Irish Bar on the *Stena Hibernia*'s Deck 5 was always a popular meeting place with its live traditional music. *(Miles Cowsill)*

*Darnia*, and *Horsa* stood in for her until she returned to service on 19th March.

In April 1990 the 'hostile bid' for Sea Containers was finally resolved, the container business going to Tiphook for £321m and Sealink British Ferries to Stena for £259m. The company would now be known as Sealink Stena Line (SSL), thus keeping the brand name to the fore for the time being. The new owners quickly announced plans for a £178m fleet-wide and infrastructure investment programme which included the port of Holyhead. The *St Columba* would receive a £6m rebuild of her passenger accommodation, designed to bring her into line with Stena's much vaunted 'Travel Service Concept' as applied to their Scandinavian ferries and outlined in Chapter 1.

The ship emerged from this as the *Stena Hibernia*, reviving the traditional name, and was joined by another renamed vessel, *Stena Cambria* (ex *St Anselm* from Dover/Folkestone with her capacious freight capacity), to work in tandem and offering two extra return sailings each day. During overhauls and non-availability issues over the next two years the *Stena Horsa*, *Stena Hengist*, *Earl William* and the freighters *Cambridge Ferry* and *St Cybi* (ex S*tena Sailor*) would provide temporary cover, though by the spring of 1992 all had been disposed of as a result of 'Operation Benchmark'. This came about as a result of a disastrous first trading year for Stena, whose UK operation had made a pre-tax loss of £28.2m. For the 1992/3 winter it was the French registered *Chartres* which covered refits on the Dun Laoghaire service, though 1993 was to be her Sealink swansong, being sold in the November to Agapitos Line, Piraeus, Greece and renamed *Express Santorini*.

By 1993 it appeared that the economies brought about by Operation Benchmark were now beginning to have an effect with Sealink Stena Line now on a better financial footing. A number of developments were beginning to materialise at Holyhead including the introduction that June of a high-speed car ferry operation from there to Dun Laoghaire, which would almost halve the crossing time to 110 minutes. The InCat Tasmanian built 74m wave-piercing catamaran, cleverly named *Stena Sea Lynx* would bring a totally new concept of travel to the Irish Sea. The bridge crew would consist of Master, Navigator, Chief Engineer and Assistant Engineer, together with four deck crew to moor and supervise the loading of the 90-car capacity vehicle deck. The craft had accommodation for 450 passengers and was run much on the

Observed in March 1989 at Holyhead's Salt Island berth whilst covering refits the French train ferry *Saint Eloi*'s internal condition drew many complaints. *(Ferry Publications Library)*

Viewed departing Holyhead in 1991, the *Earl William*'s last few months of Sealink service were spent on the Dun Laoghaire route. *(Miles Cowsill)*

lines of an aircraft with a cabin manager overseeing around 10 cabin crew who would demonstrate safety procedures, run the shop, bar and café as well as clean the craft during turnround times. For passenger comfort the craft would not

*Stena Cambria*, now in the Stena Sealink Line (1992) branding, backs towards the Salt Island berth at Holyhead after crossing from Dun Laoghaire. *(Miles Cowsill)*

be allowed to operate in winds above Force 7 or in wave heights exceeding 3.5m.

For the following year Stena Sealink Line leased a second and larger 81m InCat, the *Stena Sea Lynx II* (612 passengers and 135 cars) from the same source, the *Stena Sea Lynx* transferring to the southern corridor route from Fishguard to Rosslare. Notwithstanding improvements in both ride control and reliability one of the secrets of Stena Sealink Line's success was to run these craft alongside the conventional ferries so that if for any reason the fast craft was off service then customers would have an alternative.

## The HSS Beckons

Hard on the heels of the news regarding the *Stena Sea Lynx's* UK arrival came the momentous announcement that Stena Line had placed an order with Finnyards, Rauma, Finland, initially for two (but later three) £65m giant High-

The *Stena Sea Lynx II* reverses from her berth at Dun Laoghaire in 1994. This was her one and only season on the Irish Sea. *(Miles Cowsill)*

The town and hills behind Dun Laoghaire make an excellent backdrop as the *Stena Hibernia*, also sporting the Stena Sealink Line branding, exits the harbour bound for Holyhead. *(Miles Cowsill)*

Speed Sea Service catamarans (HSS). The first craft was slated to go into service on the Holyhead-Dun Laoghaire route as from 1995, the others on routes at the time not yet decided, but soon afterwards being announced as from Stranraer to Belfast and Hoek van Holland to Harwich. If anything was to be a game changer, then this was to be it!

In order to accommodate the new HSS craft at Holyhead and Dun Laoghaire a great deal of building work was needed at both ports. At Holyhead, the old station berth was closed and a new link bridge constructed to connect the east and west sides of the Inner Harbour. This resulted in the *Stena Hibernia* and *Stena Cambria* having to use the original car ferry berth at Salt Island, whilst at Dun Laoghaire, St Michael's Pier was being totally revamped, fronted by a large landscaped plaza to welcome travellers.

The revolutionary 40 knot HSS craft would dwarf any previous fast craft, measuring 19,638gt, 140m in length, 40m in the beam and be able to accommodate 1500 passengers, 375 cars or a combination of 50 lorries and 100 cars. Loading

and unloading would be by special stern ramps with turnround times being envisaged at a mere 30 minutes. Internally, the open-plan passenger areas would be very much in line with marine architect's Figuara's shopping mall concepts. The HSS would be powered by 4 General Electric gas-turbine engines adapted for marine use, Stena Line had very wisely taken the precaution of investing in a 10-year agreement for gas oil at 1995 prices, though in the end the astronomic rise in fuel costs during the next decade would be the undoing of this futuristic piece of technology. Over the next three years the HSS was constructed in great secrecy, the inevitable technical delays meaning that the *Stena Explorer*, as she was now named, didn't make her debut to the press off Dover until rather later than planned on 20th February 1996.

**Holyhead-Dublin Debut**

Almost passing under the radar on 13th October 1995, the small ro-ro ferry *Marine Evangeline* began a new freight

Two impressive views of the HSS *Stena Explorer*. The top view shows her as she begins to accelerate away from Holyhead, note the rolling effect this has on the water. The right hand view sees her laid up at Holyhead after the last sailing of the day from Ireland. *(Miles Cowsill/Gordon Hislip)*

Another image of the *Stena Hibernia*, this time at the Salt Island berth, Holyhead, with her bow visor raised to produce a through flow of air before loading recommences. *(Miles Cowsill)*

The *Stena Traveller* at Holyhead's new outer berth. Introduced in late 1995 the ship successfully built up traffic on the new Dublin freight service. *(Miles Cowsill)*

service from Holyhead to Dublin. This was a precursor to the ro-pax vessel *Stena Traveller* with its ability to carry up to 100 commercial vehicles taking up service on 2nd November 1995. Her arrival gave hauliers their own dedicated freight ship with two round trips a day, much to the pleasure of locals at Dun Laoghaire as it took a great deal of the heavy lorry traffic away from the town. The new venture would eventually morph into the very successful operation Stena has with its giant superferries on the Holyhead-Dublin service today.

In September 1995 the process began of removing the privatised Sealink branding ('galloping maggots' and all) from the funnels in favour of the parent company's smart new Stena Line livery, the *Stena Challenger* at Dover being the first to receive it. The corporate rebranding designed by Landor Associates officially came into use on 1st January 1996. Stena's existing funnel livery was slightly modified, blue replacing the black at the base, with the previous gold hull lettering and stripes replaced by more vibrant blue lettering and red stripes.

61

In September 1996 the *Stena Traveller* was replaced by her near sister vessel *Stena Challenger* which, with her increased passenger capacity, allowed motorists to travel. Seen here departing Dublin for Holyhead. *(Miles Cowsill)*

Repainted in the 1996 Stena Line livery, the *Stena Cambria* manoeuvres away from the berth at Dun Laoghaire. *(Miles Cowsill)*

Receiving her new livery during her winter refit at Swansea the *Stena Hibernia* returned with a new name - *Stena Adventurer*. This name change was in anticipation of a possible transfer to Dover in order to make use of her passenger capacity there once the HSS *Stena Explorer* had settled in on her Irish Sea service. In the event she remained at Holyhead supporting the HSS.

An unusual visitor to the Irish Sea between February and April 1996 was the much-travelled *Stena Londoner* (ex *Versailles*), which had just been displaced from the Newhaven-Dieppe route. She covered refits at both Fishguard and Holyhead and was serving at the latter port in the days leading up to the *Stena Explorer* beginning her official service.

Arriving at Holyhead on 21st February 1996 the *Stena Explorer* spent the next few weeks further fitting out and undergoing safety tests with both the UK's Department of Transport (DOT) and Irish Marine. Her 'Maritime and Coastguard Agency Permit to Operate' would initially only allow her to sail in waves of up to four metres significant

In 1996 the 'Hibernia' was renamed as the *Stena Adventurer* in anticipation of a possible transfer to Dover once the HSS *Stena Explorer* had settled in. This did not happen and she was withdrawn from service in the late October. *(Miles Cowsill)*

height, so her first sailings were restricted to 2.6m wave heights by the DOT pending a bad weather testing of the new marine evaluation system. Rather than take the HSS out of service, the system was refitted onto the *Stena Galloway* from Stranraer for a final evacuation test and received approval from both the British and Irish authorities. Finally, on 10th April 1996 the *Stena Explorer* made her debut.

An instant success, the *Stena Explorer* carried 36,000 passengers and 6,000 vehicles in her first week in service, reaching a zenith of 1.7m passengers carried in 1998. With up to five round trips each day she boosted the day trip options for both passengers and cars.

*A more comprehensive description of the HSS and the technology behind it is to be found in Chapter 4 - Innovative HSS.*

The entry into service of the *Stena Explorer* meant that the *Stena Adventurer's* days on the Holyhead-Dun Laoghaire route were now coming to an end, especially as her possible move to Dover had been dropped. On 30th September at the

end of the summer season and some six months after the high-speed craft's entry into service, the *Adventurer* was put on standby at the Carlisle Pier, Dun Laoghaire. She did one last round trip clearing a back log of traffic on 29th October before later sailing from Dun Laoghaire to Belfast for lay-up and sale. The event did not go unnoticed, with vessels and vehicles of all shapes and sizes sounding their horns in salute to a much-loved ship.

She remained in Belfast throughout the winter but in Spring 1997 news came that she had been sold to Agapitos Express Ferries, Greece, formally being handed over at their *Express Aphrodite* on 9th May. She still trades today as the *Masarrah,* registered in Saudi Arabia, operating across the Red Sea on the pilgrim trade between Duba and Safaga for Namma Shipping Lines.

The *Stena Cambria* returned to Holyhead in April 1997 to cover for the refit of the HSS making her final crossing to Dun Laoghaire on 3rd May, this being the last ever conventional ferry sailing from the Irish port. By then the *Stena Cambria*

A rare image of the *Stena Challenger* approaching Cork in July 1996, having been chartered by the 'Tour de France' organisation to take support teams and their equipment from there to Roscoff for the next stage of the race. *(Ferry Publications Library)*

The *Stena Forwarder* was chartered in 2001 to replace the *Stena Challenger* on the Holyhead-Dublin service. Whilst impressive in her all-white hull and red Stena Line funnel, she lacked bow thrust power which led to protracted berthing issues. Here she is preparing to berth at Dublin. *(Miles Cowsill)*

was leading a very peripatetic life with stints at Stranraer, Newhaven and Dover, withdrawal from service coming in early February 1999. Sold to Umafisa, Ibiza, Spain and renamed *Isla de Botafoc* for services between Ibiza and Barcelona, she is still in active service today as the *Bari* for Ventouris Ferries between Durres (Albania) and Bari (Italy).

Moving back to September 1996, the *Stena Challenger* had been released from her Dover-Calais duties to replace her near sister *Stena Traveller* on the Holyhead-Dublin freight route, the latter returning to Stena's Baltic services. Earlier in the July, she had been specially chartered by the 'Tour de France' organisation to take support teams and their equipment from Cork (Ireland) to Roscoff (France). En-route to Holyhead she refitted at Falmouth, work which included the fitting of a new stern ramp for her role on the Irish Sea. Her first crossing to Dublin was on 17th September and with her passenger certificate for 500, twice that of her sister, it allowed accompanied car traffic to be carried on her twice

A view across Holyhead Harbour from the bridge of the *Stena Forwarder* with Irish Ferries' *Ulysses* in the background. *(Miles Cowsill)*

Observed berthing at Dublin, the *Stena Adventurer* (2003) is a massive 43,532gt ro-pax vessel able to carry 210 lorries or 640 cars as well as 1,500 passengers. Her introduction on the Holyhead-Dublin service has substantially enabled the operation to grow. *(Miles Cowsill)*

www.stenaline.com

Stena Line

daily schedule between the two ports. The *Challenger* continued to build up traffic on the route remaining there until April 2001 when she was purchased by the Canadian Government for Marine Atlantic, renamed *Leif Ericson* for services between New Sydney (Nova Scotia) and Port Aux Basques and Argentia (Newfoundland).

On the refit front December 1999 saw the ex-Dover ferry *Stena Invicta* at Holyhead covering on the Dun Laoghaire service.

**An Adventurous Superferry Arrives**

The *Stena Challenger's* replacement was the brand-new Italian Visentini ro-pax vessel *Stena Forwarder* which Stena had chartered on an initial two-year contract. She looked impressive in her all-white hull and red Stena Line funnel and, whilst her arrival was seen as a relatively short-term measure until new purpose-built tonnage came into service, she did enable business to further grow on the Dublin route. Being Italian flagged, the *Forwarder* had Italian Captains, together with a British Captain on board as 'the owner's representative'.

Measuring 25,000gt and 186m in length and with a service speed of 24 knots this enabled her to cross in 3 hours, some 45 minutes quicker than the *Stena Challenger.* She could accommodate 1,000 passengers and with 2,100 lane metres of space available could carry up to 140 lorries, some 60% more than her predecessor. On the downside, the *Stena Forwarder* rather lacked bow thrust power which in high winds often meant protracted berthing issues, rather mitigating the time gains she made on the open sea. In 2003 Stena announced that one of the new builds on order from Hyundai Heavy Industries, Ulsan, South Korea would replace her on the Dublin route and be named *Stena Adventurer*. On 13th April 2003, the *Stena Forwarder* made her final crossing, immediately being chartered to Baja Ferries, Mexico who renamed her *California Star* and subsequently purchased the ship in 2007.

In the four-month interim period preceding the *Stena Adventurer's* arrival on the scene in July 2003, the route was covered by the veteran *Stena Transporter* which was normally to be found on the Harwich-Europoort freight route.

As for the *Stena Adventurer*, she was huge and at 43,532gt, 211m in length and with a service speed of 22 knots was a

The Stena *Adventurer* powers her way towards Dublin Port; she can load on two decks simultaneously, though being a ro-pax her outside deck space is more limited. *(Miles Cowsill)*

Whilst not the largest vessel in the Stena fleet, the *Stena Nordica*, is one of the most versatile and valued; viewed here arriving at Dublin. *(Gordon Hislip)*

match for the Irish Ferries' flagship *Ulysses* on the same routing. With twin KaMeWa controllable-pitch propellers, dual Becker rudders and KaMeWa bow thrust units she quickly gained a reputation for being a very manoeuvrable ferry. Costing some £60m her passenger certificate was for 1500 persons (up by 50%) and she could load bow and stern simultaneously on two levels with 3,400 lane metres available for either 640 cars or 210 lorries (an increase of 70% per sailing) or a mixture of the two.

The *Stena Adventurer* offered very spacious passenger accommodation with a 'Globetrotter' Restaurant and Bar, 'Rudi's Diner', 'Stena Plus Lounge', children's play area, cinema/conference room and casino.  For drivers there was a 'Truckers Lounge' together with 148 cabins for 364 guests. As with any ro-pax ship of this type outside deck space tends to be relatively limited.

By 2006 business on the route had grown significantly enough for Stena Line to introduce their freight ship *Stena*

Captured in the early morning light at Dublin, the *Stena Adventurer* is about to set off for Holyhead. *(Matt Davies)*

*Seatrader* which had previously served on the Harwich/Killingholme-Hoek of Holland routes for many years but was now being displaced by new tonnage. Her schedule, initially for one round trip per day, thus further increased the capacity and marked the beginning of moves towards having two 'superferries' on the Dublin service. She remained on the route until the end of 2008 when sold as the *Seatrade* to Ventouris Ferries for further service on their routes out of Bari to Igoumenitsa (North West Greece) and Durres (Albania).

In the '*Seatrader's*' place, in November 2008, came the *Stena Nordica* (ex *European Ambassador*) which had been operating on Stena's Poland to Sweden routes. Dating from 2000, this ro-pax was a much more modern vessel, measuring 24,206gt, 170m with a service speed of 25 knots. She had a passenger certificate for 420 and could accommodate 375 cars and with 1,900 lane metres available for freight, the equivalent to 90 lorries. The following year in March 2009 she received a major refit and refurbishment including a Stena Plus Lounge, Food City restaurant and a new freight drivers' area.

For the *Stena Explorer* rising fuel costs of $110 for a barrel of crude in 2008, from the mere $16 in 1994 when the craft was being designed (n.b. $56 in 2020), began to adversely affect its financial viability. During the winter of 2008 the

In 2006 Stena Line introduced second freight ship, *Stena Seatrader,* on the Holyhead-Dublin route. She had previously served on the Harwich/Killingholme-Hoek of Holland services. Pictured here rounding Poolbeg Lighthouse on her way into Dublin. *(Gordon Hislip)*

Preceding the *Stena Adventurer*'s arrival in 2003, the Harwich freighter *Stena Transporter* covered on the Holyhead-Dublin freight service, seen here departing Dublin. *(Gordon Hislip)*

In early 2013 the *Finnarrow* was chartered from Finnlines to cover refits on the Central Corridor. Here she makes her way into Dublin Port. *(Gordon Hislip)*

vessel would only make one return crossing a day, except over the Christmas and New Year period when three round trips would still be on offer. More ominously for the HSS, for the first time Stena Line were now accepting foot passengers in addition to those travelling by car on their Holyhead-Dublin service. It was also planned to slow the *Stena Explorer* by 16 minutes in order to reduce fuel costs.

Six years down the line in 2009 the *Stena Adventurer* received a well-deserved £3.1m internal revamp with the introduction of the very successful 'Stena Plus Lounge' concept incorporating a family area, a new 'Business Lounge' with Wi-Fi, 'Barista Coffee Outlet', 'Teen Town' (including MSM stations) as well as a quiet reading room. Today, she has been further revamped to bring her facilities and branding in line with those of her running partner, *Stena Estrid* on the Dublin service *(see below)*.

More scaling down of the *Stena Explorer's* schedules were put in place for her 2010 season, being replaced in the off-peak periods by the 81m *Stena Lynx III* which was a significantly cheaper craft to operate. The *Explorer's* peak summer season was scheduled to run from the end of June until the beginning of September but returned to service earlier than originally planned, following an upswing in the number of bookings. The *Stena Lynx III* moved to Fishguard for her summer operations to Rosslare as planned.

## Superfast time

The *Stena Nordica* would remain on the Holyhead-Dublin route until March 2015 (other than when covering for refits at Cairnryan and Fishguard) when she was superseded by the *Stena Superfast X*. Very much one of the versatile workhorses of the Stena fleet, since then the *Nordica* has seen charter work with DFDS (2015) on their Dover-Calais services as the *Malo Seaways* and, having resumed her Stena name, for Grandi Navi Veloci (GNV) on their routes between Palermo (Sicily) and the Italian mainland in 2016. Later that year she returned to the Stena fold on their Baltic services as well as continuing to cover for refits at Fishguard (*Stena Europe*) and Rosslare (*Stena Horizon*) in 2017 and again in 2019 whilst the *Stena Europe* was on an extended refit.

Moving ahead, at the beginning of May 2020 and having just finished a charter contract with the UK's Department of

This imposing three-quarter bow shot of the *Stena Superfast X* amply demonstrates her powerful qualities as she approaches Dublin. *(Gordon Hislip)*

Transport the *Stena Nordica* was brought in to relieve the *Stena Estrid* on the Holyhead-Dublin route, the E-Flexer experiencing mechanical issues. She took up her Irish Sea sailings on 3rd May with the 08.55 service from Holyhead to Dublin. Once the *Stena Estrid* returned the *Stena Nordica* was expected to cover for the *Stena Europe* on the Fishguard-Rosslare service during the latter's scheduled maintenance period. Afterwards, the ship would return to Poland to take up her scheduled services from there to Sweden. Whilst she is not the largest vessel in the Stena fleet, she is one of the most versatile and valued being a real 'go anywhere' workhorse.

The 30,285gt *Superfast X*, as she was originally named, dates from February 2002, and was 204m in length and as her names suggests very fast at 28.5 knots, though in practice 22 knots was her normal operating speed. She had a passenger certificate for 1,200 and space for 480 cars or 110 trucks or a mixture of the two. Being designed primarily as a night-ship she originally had 364 cabins, though with subsequent modifications to suit the needs of different operators this number rather varied. She was first employed on the company's short-lived Superfast Hanko (Finland)-Rostock (Germany) route, which lasted a mere seven weeks before commencing operations in UK waters in the May on their

The Stena *Superfast X* has operated throughout Europe. After purchasing her in 2014 Stena revamped her into an excellent vessel suited for the Dublin-Holyhead service. With the arrival of the *Stena Estrid* in 2020, she has since been chartered for services in the Mediterranean. *(Miles Cowsill)*

Rosyth-Zeebrugge service.

In 2007, she was sold to the French company Veolia Transport for around £85m and renamed *Jean Nicoli* for services in the Mediterranean. Again, this was short-lived as in 2008 she was sold to SeaFrance for their Calais-Dover crossing as the *SeaFrance Moliere.* Her refurbishment to make her suitable for this 90-minute crossing saw many of her cabins being removed and being almost completely refigured. Following the liquidation of SeaFrance in late 2011 she was sold to Scapino Shipping and laid up at Tilbury. It took until November 2012 before she found new work, DFDS chartering her to serve on the same short-sea crossing renamed as their *Dieppe Seaways.*

It was at the end of this charter in 2014 that Stena took possession of the vessel returning her to her original name, albeit with a Stena prefix. They then sent her for an extensive refit to bring the ship configuration, interiors and facilities back into line with sisterships on the () to route. Having operated for no less than 7 different operators in the Baltic, North Sea, Mediterranean, English Channel and now finally the Irish Sea, there was much work to do!

Stena believed that the ship would prove ideal for the Irish Sea in an expanding market, especially with her ability to carry 4.65m high trailers. Operating in tandem with the *Stena Adventurer* she offered two return crossings each day (Dublin Port at 02.12 and 15.10 with returns from Holyhead at 0.855 and 20.30).

The *Stena Explorer* completed her 2014 summer season on 9th September with the expectation that she would return in the following year. However, in February 2015, came the news from Stena Line that the HSS would be withdrawn from the Dun Laoghaire route with immediate effect, and in future all services would now be from Holyhead to Dublin.

It was the end of a wonderful era for the HSS which during its peak in 1998 was carrying over 1.7m passengers per year, but by 2014 this had shrunk to a mere 200,000 which had made the route unsustainable. Changes in travelling habits, more attractive conventional ferries, competition from airlines, rampaging increases in fuel costs and a consequent reduction in frequencies all contributed to its demise. Somehow the ferry world seemed a little less exciting.

Ian Davies, Stena Line's Route Manager (Irish Sea South) commented: 'Whilst the HSS class was a unique and highly

73

Stena elegance; the superbly fitted out main bar area on Deck 8 of the *Stena Superfast X*. *(Stena Line)*

The spacious and comfortable family lounge on-board the *Stena Superfast* X, Deck 7. *(Stena Line)*

The *Stena Superfast X*'s very modernistic Barista Bar is located on Deck 8. *(Stena Line)*

innovative development for Stena Line at the time, the market has evolved significantly since her introduction in the mid-1990s and today's business model requires a more balanced mix of freight and car traffic all year round.

Captain Andrew Humphreys, Stena Line's Safety Manager for the UK who had the honour of bringing the vessel into Holyhead in February 1996 recalled the event vividly. 'I can remember everything about that special day. Holyhead, a port used to virtually every shape and size of vessel had never seen anything like it. The *Stena Explorer* was the most beautiful and innovative looking vessel we had ever seen and to have the opportunity to Captain this superb vessel was an honour that I will treasure for the rest of my life'.

The *Stena Explorer* was purchased by Karadeniz Powership Holdings, Yavlova, near Istanbul. Turkey as an 'earthquake resistant' floating office, research space and alternative power generator at the Karmarine Shipyard, Yalova, near Istanbul, Turkey. Renamed *One World Karadeniz*, the last of the HSS fleet left Holyhead under tow on 1st November arriving at Yalova three weeks later.

On 9th March 2015, the *Stena Superfast X* began her service on the Holyhead-Dublin route replacing the *Stena Nordica* which, paradoxically, DFDS were chartering as their *Malo Seaways* as a short term measure on the Calais-Dover route. With Stena working their magic once more when it comes to refurbishments the *Stena Superfast X* now had excellent facilities, ideal for the route. As a result, over the next five years she substantially increased the freight and passenger carryings.

The demise of the HSS service also saw the end of Dun Laoghaire as a ferry port. Although the port authority at one time said that no less than seven operators had expressed an interest there were no takers, one possible reason being that port charges were said to be around three times as much as those at Dublin. In 2017, the Dun Laoghaire Harbour Company applied for planning permission to change the use of the 1995 built ferry terminal to offices, the fast craft infrastructure having now been demolished.

With the introduction of the Stena E-Flexer, *Stena Estrid,* to the Holyhead-Dublin crossing in January 2020, the *Stena Superfast X* left Holyhead for Belfast in order to release the *Stena Superfast VII* and *Stena Superfast VIII* s. In turn, she dry-docked at Harland & Wolff before deputising for the *Stena Horizon*. As a finale the *Stena Superfast X* was then required to return to the Holyhead-Dublin service in order to release the *Stena Adventurer* for her refit at A&P Falmouth.

In early February 2020 it was announced that the *Stena Superfast X* would be chartered to Corsica Linea in a long-term arrangement with Stena RoRo, with a possible option to purchase. She was renamed *A Nepita*, and sailed to Piraeus, Greece, for a refit including the installation of an open loop type scrubber in order to reduce greenhouse gas emissions. Additionally, around 100 new cabins would be fitted (replacing those removed when she was converted to a day ship for services across the Dover Strait), together with a new reclining seat lounge in order to make her more suited on services between France and Algeria.

## Stena Estrid - flexibility in the extreme

On 16th January 2019, Stena Line's newest ferry *Stena Estrid* was christened and floated out at the China Merchants Jinling Shipyard (previously known as AVIC Weihai Shipyard Co., Ltd), in north-western China, the first in a series of E-Flexer vessels. The name Estrid is an old Norse version of Astridr and means 'Beautiful Goddess' (Ass = God; Fridr = Beautiful) and was chosen to reflect Stena Line's Scandinavian roots.

The term E-Flexer was chosen to reflect the main goals of the design, namely efficiency and flexibility, a concept known within the company as 'Stenability', reflecting their role both as innovators and informed strategic thinkers. The ships are designed to be amongst some of the most fuel efficient in the world and to be flexible enough to operate across a number of differing routes and distances.

The *Stena Estrid* (41,671gt, 212m, 1,000 passengers) commenced her sea trials on 5th September achieving an excellent 22.4 knots in the process, performing in line with the build specification, including a thorough testing of all management and safety systems. The ferry was handed over to Stena Line on schedule on 15th November and made ready for the 10,000-mile voyage to the UK, manned by a delivery crew of 27. Leaving on 22nd November, much of the voyage was at the economical speed of 17 knots using just one of her twin Caterpillar MaK 12 M43 C engines at a time, thereby saving fuel. Travelling via Singapore, Sri Lanka and the Suez

Constructing the foremast on the *Stena Estrid* at the China Merchants Jinling Shipyard, Weihai, fitting out berth. *(CMI Jinling Weihai Shipyard)*

Canal she sailed along the Mediterranean to Algeciras arriving on 19th December. There she took on additional crew members for familiarisation and training during the last leg to Holyhead. The *Stena Estrid* reached the Welsh port on the 23rd December, just in time for Christmas.

The 3,100 lane metres available on her vehicle decks enables the *Stena Estrid* to accommodate 210 lorries with space for a further 120 cars on a dedicated motorists' car deck. This represents a 50% increase in capacity over her predecessor on the route, the *Stena Superfast X*.

Stena have taken much care in ensuring that the environmental footprint has been kept to the minimum. Improvements in engine technology and underwater hull and bow design mean about 25% less $CO_2$ emissions per freight

unit than with existing ro-pax ferries. The hull of the new vessel is coated in a bio-repellent antifouling ingredient claimed to be very effective in combating build-up of marine growth, reducing drag through the water and in consequence lowering fuel consumption. Other 'green' initiatives include ensuring a significant reduction in single-use plastic, the provision of multi-recycling facilities, LED lighting and energy saving solar film on windows.

Passenger vehicles have their own dedicated garage on Deck 7 towards the stern and can walk straight into the passenger accommodation without the need to use any lifts, steps, or stairs. The only downside to this is at disembarkation in certain circumstances it may require some freight to be off-loaded first. Extra cars and freight are stowed on the *Stena*

A stunning aerial view of the *Stena Estrid* showing a largely uncluttered deck, though much work still has to be done. *(CMI Jinling Weihai Shipyard)*

Dignitaries, guests and workers assemble for the launching ceremony of the *Stena Estrid* on 16th January 2019. *(CMI Jinling Weihai Shipyard)*

The *Stena Estrid* sets off on her sea trials on 5th September, achieving an excellent 22.4 knots in the process. *(CMI Jinling Weihai Shipyard)*

*Estrid's* three other vehicle decks: Deck 1, Deck 3, and Deck 5. In addition to wheelchair ramps, the needs of those with mobility issues and of parents with buggies are aided by having the door coamings from these vehicle decks only 2-3cm in height, making them relatively easily managed.

On board there is a feeling of both lightness and spaciousness exemplified by an atrium feature together with large panoramic windows through which to watch the world go by. Passenger facilities are mostly to be found on Decks 7 and 8, with Wi-Fi available throughout the ship.

Deck 7 is home to the 'Guest Services' with the main focus on eating and retail activities including overlooking the bow the 'Taste' restaurant with seating for up to 325 people, the 'Barista Coffee House' and a 'Happy World' play area with an attached lounge for parents to relax in. The 'Outlet On-board' shop offers a range of goods including perfumes, gifts, newspapers and the like; interestingly you can self-scan your purchases if you so wish. This area also provides access to the outside promenade decks on either side of the vessel.

The deck above (Deck 8) is given over to entertainment and general relaxing. Located forward is the 'Stena Plus Premium Lounge', access is via a digital key panel and passengers are free to help themselves to a range of hot and cold drinks and snacks with a table service provided for food.

Behind this is the 'Hygge Premium Recline Lounge' for sumptuous relaxing, On the starboard side is the 170-seat 'Truckers Lounge' for freight drivers whilst on the port side are the 'Living Room' and 'News Room' lounges.

The midships area of this deck is dominated by a glass atrium which allows in lots of natural light on to the 170-seater 'Sky Bar' area. A second 'Happy World' children's play facility is provided on the port side, although being overlooked by the 'Sky Bar' it does not have its own dedicated lounge area. Further aft are two movie lounges, one on each side, both of which have three 65" screens with the seating laid out as if you are in your own home.Aft of these public areas and on Deck 9 are 175 passenger cabins including six de-luxe cabins, all with balconies. The forward part of Deck 9 contains the crew accommodation, whilst above this on Deck 10 is a large Sun Deck, though currently it lacks wind shelters and seating. It is very refreshing to find such plentiful outside deck space on a modern ferry with promenade decks on Deck 7, aft on Decks 8 and 9 as well as on the Sun Deck.

On Monday 13th January 2020, the *Stena Estrid* made her historic maiden commercial voyage, slightly delayed owing to the presence of Storm Brendan. Despite the distinctly unfavourable conditions the new ferry was said to have performed extremely well through six metre waves. She has

Dublin on 22nd December 2019 and a first arrival for berthing trials for the *Stena Estrid*, pictured here with the *Stena Superfast X* (who she replaced) passing her en-route to Holyhead. *(Gordon Hislip)*

Monday 23rd December 2019, and it's the *Stena Estrid*'s maiden call at Holyhead, typically in windy conditions with a tug on hand just in case. *(Stena Line)*

slotted into the No 1 diagram (departing Holyhead at 08.55 and 20.30, and from Dublin at 02.15 and 14.50) in place of her consort *Stena Adventurer*.

Things do not always go quite to plan, as has already been noted, at the beginning of May 2020 the new £160m super-ferry had to be taken off the Holyhead to Dublin route for repairs after suffering mechanical issues, just four months after entering service. The *Stena Nordica*, having just finished a charter contract with the UK's Department of Transport was now available and was brought in to relieve her on the Holyhead-Dublin route.

Whilst the *Stena Estrid* had been running on one engine for several weeks, she is capable of maintaining a service speed of 18 knots using one engine and one propeller and still be fully 'Safe Return to Port' compliant. With freight volumes and passenger volumes lower than usual owing to the COVID-19 Coronavirus pandemic, it was deemed an appropriate time to take the ship out of service. The vessel sailed to Cairnryan on 2nd May 2020, where the work was undertaken by Stena Line's engineers, with the ship not returning to service until mid-June.

Spacious, airy and light throughout and with a crew rightly

proud of her, the *Stena Estrid* has brought a new dimension to ferry travel across this part of the Irish Sea. Innovative, economic and flexible, the exciting times are already here!

*A further in-depth view on the E-Flexer concept can be found in Chapter 6 - Flexible Future*

Looking powerful and more than capable, the *Stena Estrid* arrives off Holyhead for the first time. *(Stena Line)*

## Earl William - Irish Sea

In December 1976 the *Viking II*, was purchased by British Rail to modernise their services between Portsmouth and the Channel Islands. Her refit at Holyhead, which included a complete mechanical rebuild, took some thirteen months before she could debut as the *Earl William* in January 1978.

Whilst it can be said that the *Earl William* began her Sealink career at Holyhead, it was not until a decade later in April 1988 that she actually sailed in service to Dun Laoghaire, albeit in a freight capacity following a fire on board the *St David*. That same month, with B+I withdrawing from their Liverpool-Dublin service in order to concentrate everything on the Holyhead route, Sealink British Ferries' saw an opportunity to start up their own service from Liverpool to Dun Laoghaire using this 1964 veteran. After an encouraging beginning in 1988, mechanical issues and falling patronage saw the route close on 9th January 1990.

Initially laid up at Milford Haven and devoid of any company markings she made several short returns to service, on charter to Belfast Ferries for their Liverpool-Belfast crossing, twice as cover for the *Stena Cambria* on the Dun Laoghaire route as well as on the Folkestone-Boulogne service. She returned to final lay-up at Milford Haven on 8th July 1990 and offered for sale.

Top left: Final departure from Liverpool on 9th January 1990. *(Ferry Publications Library)*

Top right: Departing Dun Laoghaire. *(Miles Cowsill)*

Centre: At Carlisle Pier, Dun Laoghaire. *(Miles Cowsill)*

Lower Right: Arriving at Liverpool. *(Miles Cowsill)*

Following the closure of the Liverpool-Dun Laoghaire service in January 1990, the *Earl William* was laid up at Milford Haven, pending charter work. *(Miles Cowsill)*

Looking aft along the *Earl William*'s pleasant portside walkway. *(Miles Cowsill)*

Milford Haven, Spring 1990 and a trio of laid up ferries; *Cambridge Ferry*, *St Cybi* (bridge just visible) and *Earl William*. *(Miles Cowsill)*

FOUR

# Innovative HSS

## The Concept

The genesis of the High-speed Sea Service (HSS) craft for Stena Line can be traced back before the early 1990s, the concept arousing much excitement amongst both ferry operators and the travelling public. Previous to this the first high-speed craft were often  or , but during the 'nineties' a new generation of wave-piercing catamaran and  designs had now become the norm. Initially there were a variety of constructors, but gradually two Australian companies,  of Perth and  of Hobart cornered much of the market.

Having carefully observed the operational capabilities of these craft, in 1993 Stena Sealink Line dipped their toes into water when chartering a 74m InCat craft from Buquebus SA of Montevideo, Uruguay, for the summer on the Holyhead-Dun Laoghaire route. The craft would have a capacity for 450 passengers, 90 cars and with a service speed of 35 knots, could, in theory, come close to halving the journey time taken by a conventional ferry. Named *Stena Sea Lynx* she was an instant success, particularly as her service was not a 'stand-alone' but complemented the conventional ferry, *Stena Hibernia*.

Whilst the *Stena Sea Lynx* and her consorts had speed there were still doubts as to their technical reliability and limited weather capabilities. Neither did they have the passenger and heavy vehicle capacity, something that Stena desired. Even before that first 1993 summer season had finished came a momentous announcement that Stena Line had placed an order with Finnyards, Rauma, Finland, initially for two (but later three) £65m giant catamarans, the first of which would to go into service on the Holyhead-Dun Laoghaire route as from 1995. This revolutionary fast craft would not just take passengers, cars and light vans, but could also accommodate heavy goods vehicles as on a conventional

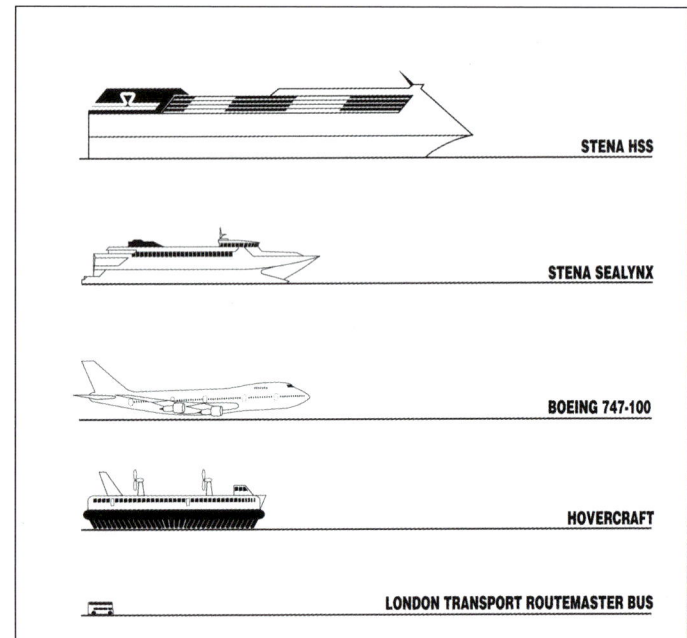

A publicity poster showing the physical size of the HSS compared to other transport icons. *(Stena Line)*

ferry. This was a very bold expression of faith in an untried design, but nevertheless very much in keeping with the Stena culture of innovation. If anything was to be a game changer, then this was it!

This revolutionary 40 knot HSS would dwarf any previous fast craft, measuring 19,638gt, 140m in length, 40m in the beam and be able to accommodate 1500 passengers, 375 cars or a combination of 50 lorries and 100 cars. Loading and unloading from very ingeniously laid out vehicle decks would be via the stern with turnround times envisaged at a mere 30

The scale models clearly showing just how big the HSS is in relation to an articulated lorry. *(Stena Line)*

The workforce are seemingly dwarfed as one of the giant 1.6m water jets is about to be fitted to the *Stena Explorer*. *(Stena Line)*

Plenty of scaffolding surrounds this HSS, showing that whilst now afloat it is still a long way off completion. *(Stena Line)*

The *Stena Explorer* is guided to her berth in the icy waters of Gothenburg prior to being formally handed over at Stena's home city on 16th February 1994. *(Stena Line)*

Judging by the crowds wishing to visit the *Stena Explorer* on the Open Day at Gothenburg it was quite a sensational debut. *(Stena Line)*

minutes. The HSS design was advanced in every respect with the passenger areas very much open plan in a further development of Stena's interior designer Figura's shopping mall concepts.

Having identified the three routes on which the HSS would operate (Holyhead-Dun Laoghaire; Stranraer-Belfast; Hoek van Holland-Harwich) a great deal of building infrastructure was required at all six ports as these vessels would not able to operate from a conventional linkspan.

The first ship of the HSS 1500 class (the name reflecting the passenger capacity) was the *Stena Explorer*, which entered service between Holyhead and Dun Laoghaire on 10th April 1996, but strangely was not formally named in Dun Laoghaire until 14th September. The second ship of the class was the *Stena Voyager*, which commenced sailing from Stranraer to Belfast on 21st July that same year. The third craft, *Stena Discovery* began her Hoek van Holland to Harwich service on 3rd June 1997.

Very much driven from the top by Sten Olsson, Stena Line's Chairman, who stated that it would 'deliver a revolution not seen since air travel moved on from the propeller to the jet age', the project was seen by many as a vote of confidence

An impressive image of the *Stena Explorer* in blustery conditions off Dover for her UK debut to the press on 20th February 1996. The *Stena Challenger* provides an excellent backdrop. *(Stena Line)*

The Motorists' Club Bar was located forward on the starboard side offering comfortable seating with front facing sea views.*(Stena Line)*

A number of the food and drink outlets were franchised, this one was operated by Ben and Jerry's. *(Stena Line)*

In this outstanding aerial view the *Stena Explorer* is carefully negotiating the narrow confines of the inner harbour at Holyhead bound for Dun Laoghaire. *(Stena Line)*

Looking aft along the starboard seating area of the Stena Explorer with, behind, the raised platforms housing the main dining outlets. (*Matt Davies)*

by Stena in the potential of their Irish Sea routes. Over the next two years the HSS was constructed amidst great secrecy, the inevitable technical delays in construction meaning that the first craft would not be ready for the 1995 summer season. The inauguration would have to wait until the following year as the icing up of the Baltic Sea each winter would preclude any travel by this non-ice class vessel.

The *Stena Explorer's* delivery voyage from Finland in February 1996, initially through the melting Baltic Sea ice and later in gale force winds from the north as she approached the Straits of Dover, was an excellent opportunity to test the craft's sea-going qualities. She passed these with flying colours making her debut to the press off Dover on 20th February.

On the technical side HSS's power plant consisted of 4 General Electric gas turbines rebuilt for maritime use, two in each hull on a 'father and son' principle, the larger one able to develop around 30,000hp at 3,600 rpm, with the smaller unit developing around 20,000hp at 6,500 rpm. Light diesel oil

The container cranes at Harwich International Port provided a good vantage point to observe the *Stena Discovery* arriving with her HSS services from Hoek van Holland. *(John Bryant)*

The *Stena Explorer* slows down as she approaches Holyhead at the end of another dash from Dun Laoghaire. *(Matt Davies)*

With the beautiful Loch Ryan shore in the background, the *Stena Voyager* prepares to berth at Stranraer. *(Matts Brevik)*

with a low sulphur content was used to power the turbines which are encased in fire and soundproof modules. The smaller of the gas turbines were adaptations of Swedish Air Force's Saab Grippen fighter plane, whilst the larger ones were used in the long-haul Boeing 747 aircraft. Such power sources are cleaner than diesel engines, use less space, are smaller and weigh less, creating a corresponding increase in the vessel's loading capacity. Above all, such plants had a high record of reliability. The downside was that they were very thirsty, a situation that has vexed the maritime world, especially with naval craft. Stena Line had very wisely taken the precaution of investing in a 10-year agreement for gas oil at 1995 prices, though in the end the astronomic rise in fuel costs during the next decade would be a major factor in the undoing of this futuristic piece of technology.

When operating in confined waters the two smaller engines were used for speeds of up to 25 knots, whilst when used together the two main turbines could raise this to around 32 knots. Using all four units, speeds in excess of 40 knots were easily attainable. Indeed, on one of the early sailings of the *Stena Explorer* in April 1996 whilst en-route to Ireland she achieved 47.8 knots (55 mph), crossing the Irish Sea in 94 minutes! The water jets were not only more efficient at high speeds but also improved manoeuvrability and markedly reduced the vessel's draft which meant less power was required to maintain the speed through the water. The water jets, with the impeller (propeller) located inside, suck in water through inlets in the ferry's hull, the largest being 1.6m in diameter. Each water jet unit was five metres long, with at the rear the steering and reversing drives, each being able to turn 30 degrees either way, thus steering the ferry in the desired direction.

With turnround times of just 30 minutes to load, unload, restock and clean the craft, innovative ways of achieving this had to be thought through. As the HSS reversed on to the berth, guided by GPS accurate to within one metre, once It made contact with the linkspan's fendering, automatic couplings on either side of the stern pulled it into the correct position in order for the locking pin to go in, ensuring a perfect fit for the vehicle and passenger gangways. The ferry's specially designed aft fender also prevented the vessel from moving sideways so no extra moorings were needed. The linkspan itself, more of a concourse, was designed with quick

couplings to facilitate fuel, freshwater replenishment and waste-water removal. Time was money so every minute of delay was crucial as well as expensive. A ten-minute delay on the Dun Laoghaire service, for example, equated to an extra five knots in order to regain the schedule.

The craft had four stern doors for rapid loading and unloading, normally three were used for unloading whilst the fourth almost simultaneously began the process of loading, to be joined by two of the others once their vehicle decks had been cleared. Two parallel passenger gangways ensured that guests could exit and board with the minimum of fuss.

In the meantime, supplies for the on-board restaurants, bars and shopping outlet were container loaded onto the HSS by means of a hoist at the stern. They were then run along a track on top of the vessel's superstructure to be delivered to the designated place i.e. retail items through a hatch towards the stern, with restaurant needs towards the bow.

Passenger baggage was registered in a similar way to airline check-ins, bar coded for easy retrieval. Once on board you were immediately immersed into a totally new concept in terms of ferry travel. The *Stena Explorer* like its two sisters offered spacious and airy accommodation and almost vibration free travel. Even at over 40 knots there was not a great sense of speed on board, the only place that one could experience it was at the stern as the massive water jets disgorged great volumes of sea water.

The HSS had only one passenger deck, the walkways and seating areas lay along the sides of the passenger deck with panoramic windows each some 30m long and 2.5m high creating a light and airy atmosphere. The central area of the craft was in tiered layers allowing excellent views across the whole deck as well as tempting guests to take full advantage of the on-board facilities and amenities.

The aft section of the passenger deck housed the information desk, duty-free shopping and the children's activity and entertainment centre, whilst the middle section was dominated by two fast food restaurants, initially including a McDonald's. Additionally, there was a bar, a playroom for pre-school children and a massive video wall, which at the time of construction was claimed to be the largest to be found on a ship anywhere, displaying information, safety messages, sales announcements and general advertising. One downside was that with the open plan nature of the craft finding a quiet space was not always easy. Another was the lack of outside deck space, very much a source of frustration for those many passengers who liked the sea air.

Further forward was the 'Globetrotter Restaurant', 'Business Lounge and 'Service Centre' for truck drivers, who had their own restaurant and shower areas. At the bow were the 'Spikes Sports' and 'Motorists Club' bars, one on each side, with the latter having its own lounge area. Dominating it all was a gigantic panoramic window where guests could lean on the rail in front of it and enjoy the sea views as they headed at speed towards their destination.

All three routes enjoyed much initial success, but as time went on passenger travelling habits began to change mainly owing to the onset of the budget airline phenomena and in particular for the HSS the rising cost of fuel which led to both the slowing down of the craft as well as reductions in service frequency.

In early 2006, Stena Line were warning that their original agreement for fuel for the HSS craft would come to an end with the company having to pay the current market costs. These had escalated to such a degree from around $16 per barrel when the craft first came into service to approaching $100 per barrel. Services would have to either pay their way or risk facing closure. The Harwich-Hoek van Holland service was said to be the most vulnerable and if this happened then Stena would be left with not just the disposal of the craft but also of the specialised infrastructure for which buyers were unlikely to be found.

### Stena Discovery

The first of the HSS craft to be withdrawn from service was the *Stena Discovery*, which only had a short life on the Hoek van Holland-Harwich route from June 1997 through to January 2007. As the other two HSS craft feature in other chapters of the book I have taken the liberty to tell the story of the *Stena Discovery* in greater detail.

Launched at the Rauma shipyard on 14th December 1996, she departed from there as scheduled on 18th April 1997. She travelled to Stockholm where she was put on show to the public, before being formally handed over to her Dutch managers Stena Line BV, Hoek Van Holland.

Her first commercial sailings were not on the Hoek van

Holland-Harwich service but from Stranraer to Belfast covering for the *Stena Voyager* from 26th April through to 24th May. Thus, it was not until 2nd June that she was able to start on her intended route. Three round trips per day were on offer with the HSS intended to replace the two older conventional overnight-ferries *Stena Europe* and *Koningin Beatrix*. Huge changes had to be made to the docking arrangements at both ports, costing around £60 million, roughly the same price as for the ship itself.

From the outset the new craft made a big impression in Holland where there had been the publicity campaign promoting her as a cost saver. However, on 4th January 1998 whilst travelling at full speed in choppy conditions the *Stena Discovery* hit a freak rogue 3.5m high wave which pushed up the nose of the ship and ripped through its underside damaging it extensively. The *Stena Voyager* temporarily replaced the HSS while it was out of action being repaired. In order to prevent this happening again small holes were created on the underside of the nose of the *Stena Discovery* to dissipate the pressure of the water, with no further recorded incidents as a result.

There were also problems ashore with people alleging that waves up to half a metre high were washing over the foreshore off Felixstowe as the craft accelerated upon exiting Harwich Haven. Nicknamed 'The Wave Machine' by the locals, Stena Line responded by agreeing to sail the ship more slowly past Harwich and Felixstowe and not accelerating to high-speed until the HSS had reached designated open water. Signs were added along the Felixstowe foreshore and a warning signal was put into place so people would know when the *Stena Discovery* was entering port. At the Hoek van Holland, residents there also got into the act by complaining about the smell from the ship's exhausts.

In March 2001 on a routine sailing a driver of an 18-ton lorry forgot to put on the handbrakes of his vehicle while parking on the vehicle deck of the ship. As the *Stena Discovery* sped up away from Hoek van Holland the lorry broke free, slid backwards, crashed through a rear door of the ferry and plunged into the water, taking three Ford Transit vans with it and, of course, the rear door. An identical incident also happened to *Stena Voyager* a number of years later on 28th January 2009 when on her way from Stranraer to Belfast.

Sadly, the HSS service on the North Sea route had not

With the Suffolk side of the River Stour behind, the *Stena Discovery* gets underway from Harwich International Port with her HSS service to Hoek van Holland. *(John Bryant)*

Window cleaning with a difference? Crew members from the *Stena Discovery* abseil down to undertake maintenance work at Hoek van Holland. *(Rob de Visser)*

really worked out and notwithstanding fuel cost issues the passenger numbers on the Hoek van Holland route were below expectation. The departure and arrival times, either very early or late, were not conducive to the travelling public, and the introduction of low-cost airline flights between Amsterdam, Rotterdam and London did not help either. In 2001 two new ro-pax ships (*Stena Hollandica* and *Stena Britannica)* were put on the route to complement the HSS and became increasingly attractive options for lorry freight and and motorists especially those with mobile homes and caravans. With an even larger *Stena Britannica* entering service in 2003 the writing was on the wall. Passenger numbers continued to decline and so it was no surprise when the *Stena Discovery* was withdrawn at the beginning of 2007. The vessel that was designed as a cost-saver had now become too expensive to operate.

After her last crossing on 8th January 2007 the *Stena Discovery* sailed for layup at Harland and Wolff, Belfast. The

A truly spectacular image of the *Stena Discovery* powering across the North Sea. *(FotoFlite)*

ship's ownership was handed back from Stena Line BV to the Stena RoRo, with the latter stating that she could not be used on Northern European services anymore, because of the design patents Stena Line possessed. Two years of idleness followed until in May 2009 she was sold to Albamar, Venezuela (where oil prices are low), and renamed *HSS Discovery* for services out of La Guaira to Estado Nueva Esparta on Margarita Island operating there for a very brief period before being taken out of service.

In November 2011, the *HSS Discovery* was moved to the Caribbean island of in an attempt to attract investors for a new ferry service from there to La Guaira. A criminal investigation shortly afterwards regarding illegal trade of diesel oil using her ballast tanks rather put paid to any thoughts of re-entry into service. In April 2015 she was sold at auction for scrapping and towed to Aliaga, Turkey, reaching there at the end of July. A sad end indeed.

## Stena Voyager

The second HSS vessel, *Stena Voyager*, entered service quite soon after the *Stena Explorer* between Belfast and Stranraer on 21st July 1996. In March 1997 she operated between Holyhead and Dun Laoghaire while the *Stena Explorer* received her first annual overhaul. Her own spring 1997 refit was covered by the brand-new *Stena Discovery* between 26th April and 24th May prior to her entering service on the North Sea.

Advertised to complete an 85-minute crossing, restrictions placed upon her by the harbour authorities at both ends of the route saw this lengthen to 105 minutes, which meant that the already tight timetables had to be adjusted accordingly. Most of her career was spent on the route, though occasionally she did cover for her sister ships when they became unavailable. In 1998, she spent over two months from 22nd of January until the 4th of April covering on the Hoek van Holland service after the *Stena Discovery* suffered damaged to her bow in rough weather. She returned to Belfast to pick up her service again as from 28th April.

Overall, she was a reliable craft with relatively few incidents, though in October 2007 a fire was discovered onboard in one of the *Stena Voyager's* engine rooms. The 601 passengers on board were issued with life jackets as the

'Voyager' made her way safely back to Belfast. The fire was extinguished by the onboard automatic systems in less than an hour and no one was injured, with the craft swiftly returning to service after inspection and repair.

On 28th January 2009, an articulated HGV lorry carrying sulphite powder became unsecured and broke free resulting in it hanging half off the stern of the craft. This prevented the craft from berthing in Stranraer harbour until a mobile crane was able to lift it off to safety. A forgotten handbrake was said to be the cause of the problem.

By 2011 the *Stena Voyager's* operational costs had risen (largely down to swingeing increases in fuel) to the point of becoming 'unsustainable'. The final nail in the *Voyager's* coffin was the decision by Stena Line to move its Scottish port of operation from Stranraer, at the bottom of Loch Ryan on the west coast, nearer to the top of the loch just north of the existing port of Cairnryan. This move was intended to save 20 minutes on the journey which meant that modern conventional ships could make the crossing almost as quickly as the HSS.

As a result the *Stena Voyager* was withdrawn from service on the 21st November 2011 to layup at the VT4 berth in Belfast. There she was joined by conventional fleetmates *Stena Caledonia* and *Stena Navigator*, also made redundant after Stena's move to the new Loch Ryan Port at Cairnryan, and replaced by the newer and more capacious conventional ferries, sisters *Stena Superfast VII* and *Stena Superfast VIII*.

The *Stena Voyager* remained at Belfast for nearly 17 months before, in April 2013, she was towed to the Öresundsvarvet Shipyard, Landskrona, Sweden, to be dismantled by Stena Line's sister company Stena Recycling Ab. who recycled everything as far as possible. Some items previously been cannibalised for use in the remaining HSS, the *Stena Explorer*.

**Stena Explorer**

And then there was one!

The *Stena Explorer* completed her 2014 summer season on 9th September with the expectation that she would return in the following year. However, in February 2015 came the news from Stena Line that the *Stena Explorer* would be withdrawn from the Dun Laoghaire route with immediate

The *Stena Voyager* turns as she prepares to berth at Stranraer during her final few days of service in November 2011. *(Miles Cowsill)*

Last days at Stranraer in November 2011, as the *Stena Voyager* sets sail to Belfast for almost one last time. *(Miles Cowsill)*

The end of the road, the *Stena Voyager* laid up at Belfast in November, 2011. She would remain there for 17 months before being scrapped. *(Author's Collection)*

The *Stena Explorer* lives on! Now the *One World Karadeniz*, an 'earthquake resistant' floating office and alternative power generator; Karmarine Shipyard, Yalova, Turkey. *(Google Earth)*

Almost for the final time, the **Stena Voyager** and **Stena Caledonia** berthed together at Stranraer in November 2011. *(Miles Cowsill)*

effect. In future all services would now be from Holyhead to Dublin.

At its peak in 1998 the *Stena Explorer* was carrying over 1.7m passengers per year, but by 2014 this had shrunk to a mere 200,000 making the route unsustainable. Whilst the HSS class was a unique and highly innovative development for Stena Line at the time, the market had evolved significantly since her introduction in the mid-1990s with today's business requiring a more balanced mix of freight and car traffic all year round.

Somehow the ferry world seemed a little less exciting. To many the *Stena Explorer* was the most beautiful and innovative looking vessel yet seen.

The *Stena Explorer* was purchased by Karadeniz Powership Holdings, Yavlova, near Istanbul, Turkey to be used as an 'earthquake resistant' floating office, research space and alternative power generator at the Karmarine Shipyard, Yalova,

near Istanbul, Turkey. Renamed *One World Karadeniz*, the last of the HSS fleet left Holyhead under tow on 1st November 2015 arriving at Yalova three weeks later.

In May 2016 she was put up for sale for £4.5m, being advertised as suitable as a floating office. 'As businesses in the Istanbul area struggle to find new space on which to build their premises, one firm has come up with a novel solution - a floating office' ran the accompanying advertising blurb. Karadeniz intimated that they had offers for the craft which they were evaluating but nothing appears to have materialised from this. Imagery on Google Earth Pro dated November 2019 shows her at the shipyard securely moored in an enclosed dock with a vehicle ramp leading to one of her stern doors, so presumably she is being used as a floating office after all!

As has been quoted before 'Loved by many and hated by some, Stena's HSS concept put new life back into travelling' - a fitting epitaph.

FIVE

# North By North West (Birkenhead/Heysham - Belfast and Fleetwood - Larne)

**The Changing Scene**

Stena Line's presence on this part of the Irish Sea, sandwiched between the Central Corridor and the North Channel, has come about in a more convoluted way. As other ferry operators have come and gone, Stena has now attained a dominant position on services from Birkenhead and Heysham to Belfast. It's a story worth telling as one tries to make sense of the events that led up to it.

When looking back over the past three decades since Stena Line arrived on the UK scene in 1990, it is only in more recent times that they have had any foothold on the ferry services across the Irish Sea from Merseyside northwards and up along the Lancashire coast to Heysham near the Cumbria border. In purchasing Sealink British Ferries, Stena Line saw an opportunity to build on those traditional Irish Sea railway served routes from Fishguard, Holyhead and Stranraer, though by then that from Heysham to Belfast had already fallen by the wayside.

The forerunners of ro-ro freight services across this stretch of water were the Atlantic Steam Navigation Company who in 1946 took the opportunity to lease war-surplus from the

ASN's *Bardic Ferry* (1957) was a trailblazer for ro-pax shipping across the Irish Sea with its superbly appointed facilities. *(Chris Howell)*

Admiralty and start the world's first freight ferry services. By 1948 the company had progressed to providing commercial services across the from Preston to Larne and Belfast. The introduction of their *Bardic Ferry* and *Ionic Ferry* in 1957 had revolutionised the market being designed to carry both passengers and vehicles as well as container traffic. The main vehicle decks were especially strengthened to take tanks in the event of the vessels being required for military service. In 1971 the company was acquired by who closed Preston, transferring the ships to their new Cairnryan-Larne.

A rain-check on ferry services as the 1980s unfolded would note that Heysham was beginning to experience the first signs of a renaissance at the port. Belfast Freight Ferries had been operating to there from Belfast since 1984, firstly with the chartered *Stena Sailor* (ex *Dundalk*), then with the *Saga Moon, Spheroid* and later the *River Lune.* At the same time the Cenargo-owned Merchant Ferries were sailing to Warrenpoint using their ro-ro freighters *Merchant Bravery, Merchant Brilliant* and *Merchant Venture.*

Further south at Fleetwood, P&O Pandoro's ships *Viking*

*Trader* and *Buffalo* were engaged on sailings to Larne. From Liverpool, Belfast Car Ferries also had a daily service to the Northern Ireland capital with their *St Colum I* and P&O Pandoro were operating a joint service with B+I to Dublin utilising their *Puma* and *Bison*. In 1988 Sealink British Ferries saw an opportunity to start up their own service from Liverpool to Dun Laoghaire using their 1964 veteran *Earl William*. After an encouraging start in 1988, mechanical issues and falling patronage saw the route closed on 9th January 1990, a few months before Stena Line formally took over that company.

Completing the picture, but out of the scope of this book, were the comings and goings of the Isle of Man Steam Packet Company which at that time were operating from Douglas to Heysham using their *Tynwald* (ex *Antrim Princess*) and freight ship *Peveril*. Today, the ro-pax *Ben-My-Chree* performs the job for both. Their side-loading ferries *Mona's Queen* and *Lady of Mann* could be seen scurrying out of Douglas on seasonal services to Fleetwood, Liverpool, Belfast and Dublin, but now there are no services to Fleetwood and any seasonal services (Liverpool being the most regular) are nearly all in the hands of their fast craft *Manannan*.

## Fleetwood

Fleetwood, at the estuary of the River Wyre, lies just north of Blackpool and is the terminus of the famous tramway. The town expanded greatly in the first half of the 20th century with the growth of the fishing industry and, although this has declined, fish processing is still a major economic activity. Today, the town's most notable employer is Lofthouse, manufacturer of the world-famous Fisherman's Friend lozenge. The port itself has had a long history of ferries particularly with those of the Isle of Man Steam Packet Company though now it is currently defunct and derelict. Fleetwood does, however, have its place in the Stena Line Irish Sea story.

A container port facility on the largely derelict Dock Street area had been created in 1973 to provide a service for goods to Larne. This ceased in 1975 when Pandoro (part of P&O European Ferries-Irish Sea) merged with Ferrymasters (Ireland) to operate a new ro-ro freight service between the two ports using their *Buffalo*, *Puma* and *Bison*. The route became

A stalwart on the Irish freight services from 1986 until 2009 the *Saga Moon* is seen at Belfast in Norfolkline livery in 2008. *(Christopher Walker)*

The *Puma* on P&O's Pandoro services between Fleetwood and Larne, later renamed *Stena Seafarer* when Stena Line took over in 2004. *(Gordon Hislip)*

financially sound, each vessel later in turn being modified in order to accommodate more freight. However, Fleetwood was very constrained by the Wyre estuary and its consequent tidal restrictions as well as by poor road communications from the M6. Finding new and suitable tonnage was always a problem, making any long-term the future for the port rather limited.

The *Saga Moon* started life in 1984 as the *Lidartindur* on freight services between the Faroe Islands and Denmark. In 1986 chartered and later sold to Belfast Freight Ferries and renamed *Saga Moon*. *(Gordon Hislip)*

In 2004 Stena Line made a bid for P&O's Liverpool-Dublin service and for the Fleetwood-Larne route. The UK Competition Commission blocked the bid for the Liverpool service but subsequently allowed Stena Line to purchase the Fleetwood-Larne route together with five ferries from P&O for £50m in cash, the transaction being completed on 5th April. The *European Leader* (ex *Buffalo*), *European Pioneer* (ex *Bison*) and *European Seafarer* (ex *Puma*) were included in the deal as were the P&O ferries from their Mostyn-Dublin route, the *European Ambassador* (later renamed *Stena Nordica*) and *European Envoy*, the latter vessel Stena Line quickly sold on to Norwegian interests. In a twist of irony all of the Fleetwood ships had been built for Stena by JJ Siestas of Hamburg West Germany in 1975 to be chartered out. In renaming them, Stena Line used the simple expedient of substituting 'Stena' for 'European'. With several reconfigurations during their three decades of service, their dimensions were somewhat varied. *Stena Leader* (12,879gt, 157m length, 17 knots, 50 passengers

The *Stena Pioneer* berthing at Larne with a full load of freight, sadly the route continued to make heavy losses and was closed in 2010. *(Miles Cowsill)*

Viewed approaching Larne, the S*tena Leader* looks very smart in her Stena Line livery. After the route closed in 2010 she was sold to Anrusstrans as their *Anna Marine*, operating between Turkey and Russia. *(Gordon Hislip)*

The *Stena Leader* and *Stena Pioneer* are pictured up for sale at Belfast in 2011 and looking rather careworn. *(Gordon Hislip)*

114 trailers; *Stena Pioneer* (14,426gt, 141.8m length, 17.7 knots, 96 passengers, 114 trailers); *Stena Seafarer* (10,957gt, 141.8m length, 18 knots, 50 passengers, 80 trailers).

Whilst it seemed surprising that Stena should want this route, it was an indication as to their longer-term strategic thinking, as freight business to Northern Ireland was on the rise. Stena's original business plan envisaged that it would be around another seven years before capital investment in new vessels would be needed. The company gave a glimpse of what could be in store for the route when they produced the aesthetically pleasing 'Stena F-Max' ferry designed to maximise the carrying capacity within the operating limits of the Lancashire port. The vessel would have a length of 170m with a draught of 4.5m and able to carry around 160 trailers with cabin accommodation for up to 500 passengers. Stena tried to breathe new life into the route but with ageing ships it was always going to be an uphill battle and losses ensued, the situation being made worse by the subsequent general economic downturn and increased competition. Investing heavily in new ships was now no longer a viable option.

Of the vessels themselves the *Stena Seafarer* seemed to be the most flexible of the trio, regularly standing in for refits and fleet unavailability at both Stranraer and Fishguard. However, it was no surprise in late 2010 to learn that the route would close at the end of that year with the loss of 140 jobs of which 62 would be at Fleetwood. The decision has probably sounded the death knell of Fleetwood as a ferry port. Driver-accompanied freight would now have to go by Stena's new Birkenhead-Belfast service, with unaccompanied trailers going via nearby Heysham to the Northern Ireland capital. Stena were at pains to point out that the decision to close had been made well in advance and was unconnected to their purchase of DFDS' Heysham-Belfast route.

Sold to Anrusstrans (Russia), but registered in Moldova and renamed *Ant 1* (*Stena Pioneer*), *Ant 2* (*Stena Seafarer*) and *Anna Marine* (*Stena Leader*) the three ex Fleetwood ships were used on services linking Guirgiulesti (Moldova), Zonguldak (Turkey) and Port Kavkaz (Russia) across the Black Sea. In late 2013 the vessels were reportedly being used to transport goods in preparation for the Sochi Winter Olympics of 2014. It was very much a 'last hurrah' as all three were beached at Aliaga in Turkey on the morning of 13th February 2014, less than a week after the Winter Olympic Opening Ceremony.

## Heysham revival

A little way up the coast from Fleetwood is Heysham, a relatively small coastal town which overlooks Morecambe Bay and the site of two nuclear power stations. Its ferry port was opened in 1904 when the Midland Railway began to operate shipping services to both Belfast and Douglas (IoM). Back in 1956 under British Railways, three newly built modern "Duke" passenger car ferries were introduced to the route – the *Duke of Lancaster*, the *Duke of Argyll* and the *Duke of Rothesay* replacing older tonnage and initially running alongside the conventional cargo vessels until 1958 when new container vessels, the *Container Enterprise* and the *Container Venturer* replaced them. At Heysham a new terminal and linkspan were built for the restyled service and, despite converting all three

into car ferries by 1970, the changes were not enough to reverse the financial losses, largely down to the increasing civil unrest in Northern Ireland and traffic levels falling markedly as a result. The railway steamer element survived through to April 1975 when the Heysham-Belfast passenger service was closed.

Later that year British Rail formed a joint venture with the P&O owned Belfast Shipping Company ro-ro freight service to Belfast under the 'Coastlink' marketing name, using their freighter *Penda*. When P&O pulled out in 1978 Sealink brought in their ro-ro *Dalriada* to the route, subsequently closing the old container operation. By 1980 the service was now in the hands of the *Lune Bridge* and *Lagan Bridge*, but with ever-increasing losses Sealink wound the route up in the December. It was not until 1999 that another passenger service to Belfast was started up by Sea Containers using their fast craft, but this was relatively short-lived, closing in 2002.

Today, Heysham, operated by Peel Ports, has begun to see a major regrowth in its fortunes handling a diverse range of general cargo and is a major offshore supply base for the Morecambe Bay gas fields. On the ferry side unaccompanied freight services to Ireland and Northern Ireland are buoyant and are now in the hands of Stena Line and Seatruck with three ro-ro ramps in use. Heysham is also the mainland ferry port for the Isle of Man Steam Packet Company with twice daily departures. In October 2016, the Bay Gateway dual carriageway from the port was opened, connecting Heysham directly to the giving a significant boost to both the town and its ferry operators.

Going back in time, in 1984 Belfast Freight Ferries began a ro-ro service for unaccompanied freight initially using the chartered *Stena Sailor,* the Northern Ireland route proving very popular with hauliers. Their success encouraged Merchant Ferries in 1986 to introduce a similar operation from Heysham to Warrenpoint, close to the Irish border but on the Northern Ireland side.

Merchant Ferries restructured their routes in 1996 and abandoned Warrenpoint making Dublin the hub for both their Heysham and Liverpool services, in doing so taking a major hold of the unaccompanied freight traffic on that part of the Irish Sea. By the turn of the century they had taken over both Norse Irish Ferries and Belfast Freight Ferries, thus operating services from Liverpool to Dublin and from Heysham to Dublin and Belfast (using their newly acquired three '*Merchants*'-

*Bravery, Brilliant* and *Venture*), becoming in turn known as Norse Merchant Ferries.

That same year, the old Warrenpoint service was restarted from Heysham by a new company made up of management displaced from the Merchant Ferries' closure there. Operating under the Seatruck banner and initially using one vessel, *Riverdance*, they are now along with Stena Line, one of the two major operators across this north-west section of the Irish Sea.

Stena Line's involvement today on the Heysham-Belfast service came as a result of acquiring the DFDS's Irish Sea Routes (who acquired them from Norfolkline, who in turn had acquired them from Norse Merchant Ferries - if you can follow the trail!) from Heysham and Birkenhead to Belfast in 2011. The two ships on the service are the *Stena Scotia* and *Stena Hibernia* which were originally Norfolkline's *Maersk Exporter* and *Maersk Importer* respectively. They date from 1996 and were built in China for Norfolkline's Scheveningen (later Vlaardingen) - Felixstowe ro-ro freight service, with two further sisters *Maersk Anglia* and *Maersk Flanders* following in 2000. Built to the 'Scheveningen max' (incidentally also the Heysham 'max') they measure 12,017gt, 142m in length, with a 18.6 knots service speed and have space for 114 trailers. Loading is on three decks, the main freight deck has a hatch with a ramp leading down to the lower hold, whilst on the port side is another ramp leading up to a partially enclosed weather deck. Being a freight-ship she is limited to 12 drivers, all of whom have their own very comfortable cabin, together with a shared dining area and separate lounge to relax in. Both these vessels have proved themselves to be an excellent acquisition.

New and larger tonnage saw them displaced on the Dutch route and in 2009 Norfolkline moved them to their Heysham-Belfast freight route. However, within a year DFDS Seaways had taken over that service, renaming them *Scotia Seaways* and *Hibernia Seaways* respectively, and repainting them in the full DFDS Seaways dark blue livery. DFDS operations were however short lived as the company quickly withdrew from the Irish Sea following a strategic review which concluded the operations were unlikely to be profitable for the foreseeable future.

Sensing an opportunity, the ever-shrewd Stena Line in 2011 purchased the DFDS services from both Heysham and Birkenhead to Belfast. Effectively, it could be said that the Heysham-Belfast route was back under the control of its antecedent owner, Sealink.

Photographed in 1997 departing Heysham, Belfast Freight Ferries' Bazias Class ferry *River Lune* looks as if a bit of 'tlc' would not go amiss. *(Simon WP)*

Norfolkline's *Maersk Exporter* (1996) was transferred from their North Sea route to Felixstowe in 2009, seen here departing Belfast for Heysham. *(Gordon Hislip)*

The two freighters were now named as *Stena Scotia* and *Stena Hibernia*, identification between them being easy in that the *Scotia* has been fitted with a rather large extension adjacent to her funnel to house the scrubber installation. Technically owned by Stena Ro-Ro and chartered back to Stena Line, at the time of writing they are the regular ships on

Norfolkline's presence on the Heysham-Belfast service was short-lived, being sold within a year to DFDS with the *Maersk Exporter* being renamed as *Scotia Seaways*. (Gordon Hislip)

this route. Between September 2012 and August 2018 Stena Line had chartered the larger capacity *Seatruck Performance* and *Seatruck Precision* (renamed as *Stena Performer* and *Stena Precision*) for the service and even having them repainted into the full Stena Line freight livery. Each vessel measured 19,772gt, 142m in length, with a 21 knot service speed. Vehicle capacity was for 140 trailers and 12 drivers could be accommodated in 6 double berth cabins.

The *Stena Hibernia* was initially chartered by SOL Continent Lines between Helsingborg-Travemünde, but this was relatively short lived and ceased in late 2012. Returning to Irish Sea service in the following year she was sent to add extra freight capacity on the Birkenhead-Belfast route operating alongside the *Stena Lagan* and *Stena Mersey,* as well as to act as refit cover for the Cairnryan vessels.

The lack of charter work for the *Stena Scotia* saw her placed into lay-up in Belfast where she remained until March 2013. She then took up a charter in the Mediterranean with CMA CGM sailing from Marseille to Oran and Mostaganem in Algeria. By September 2015 she was mainly operating on the Killingholme or Harwich to Europoort freight services.

At the end of their charter the Seatruck vessels went back to their owners, with the *Stena Scotia* joining up once more at Heysham with the *Stena Hibernia*, which had returned to the

route in 2015.

Entering and exiting Heysham presents numerous challenges to a ship's master as vessels are required to complete two 45° turns in close succession in order to pass inside the harbour entrance markers. In strong winds and or with a tide running across the harbour entrance this is no mean feat, made more so because of the huge tidal range, at low water manoeuvring in the harbour basin can be quite restrictive.

A daytime passage on a fine day between Heysham and Belfast can be a very pleasant occasion, with excellent views of a coastline rarely out of view. After proceeding out through Morecambe Bay under the backdrop of the Lake District mountains, a course is taken along the Cumbrian coast passing through several windfarms on the way. From there the ship makes for the northern tip of the Isle of Man, passing close at the Point of Ayre with views of Scotland's Galloway Peninsula on the starboard side. The Northern Ireland coastline is soon in sight with the entrance to Belfast Lough beckoning.

The route remains buoyant despite the port's limitations in terms of size of vessels that can use it. There is the possibility of a 2,700 lane metre 'Heysham Max' ro-ro ferry at some stage in the near future, and now with good access to the UK motorway system there is every good reason for this niche operation to continue to flourish.

**Belfast Bound from Merseyside**

When *Saint Columb I* was withdrawn from its Belfast-Liverpool route in October 1990 it was not entirely unexpected largely as a result of decreasing passenger numbers as the 'troubles' continued. On the positive side, there had been an increase in demand for ro-ro freight, but with the ship's capacity limited and no suitable ship seemingly available at that time the service was closed. Accompanied freight ferry services from Northern Ireland were now only from Larne to Stranraer or Cairnryan in Scotland from which initially a lengthy drive along s was necessary in order to reach the industrial centres of the North West and West Midlands in England.

Totally dissatisfied with the situation, in 1991 a joint venture between the Roed Group and a of formed their own service from Liverpool to Belfast. Known as Norse Irish Ferries, sailings

Soon after Stena Line took over from DFDS in 2012 they entered into a six year charter with Seatruck for two freighters to serve on the Heysham-Belfast service, renaming them as *Stena Performer* and *Stena Precision*. The 'Precision' is seen on weekend cover at Birkenhead for their Belfast route. *(Matt Davies)*

commenced using the *Norse Lagan* and *Transgermania* (better known as Stena Line's *Rosebay*), who were joined in 1993 by the *River Lune*. Initially they operated a freight only service, passengers later being accepted onto sailings operated by the *Norse Lagan*.

In 1995, Merchant Ferries moved their Heysham service from Warrenpoint in Northern Ireland in favour of Dublin, a move that became almost an instant success. However, it let in another company formed by the management at Warrenpoint to restart the service to Heysham. Today, Seatruck (as they became), now part of the Clipper Group, are with Stena line the prime movers of freight across this part of the Irish Sea.

Building on their own success in July 1997 Norse Irish Ferries took delivery of the first of two new built vessels from the Italian Visentini shipbuilders. These vessels were a quantum leap in ro-pax design, a winning formula that the Italian builders have continued with through to today. Named

The *Stena Scotia* (ex S*cotia Seaways*) is easily recognisable by the rather prominent scrubber arrangement on her funnel. *(Gordon Hislip)*

The *Lagan Viking*, built in Italy by Visenteni, set new standards in ro-pax operation when Norse Irish Ferries introduced her on the Liverpool-Belfast service in 1997. Her Viking sail motif and red hull reflect her part-Norwegian ownership. *(Gordon Hislip)*

*Lagan Viking* and *Mersey Viking* they had distinctive red hulls and measured 26,500gt, were 186m in length and had a service speed of 20 knots. They had a trailer capacity of 164 and a passenger/cabin certificate for 340 persons. At the same time the company introduced a new branding featuring a Viking ship sail motif reflecting the Norwegian partners in the company.

In 1999 Merchant Ferries also had expansion plans with a new route from Liverpool to Dublin in competition with the existing P&O Irish Sea Freight. New ships were ordered for the service from Astilleros Espanoles SA (AESA), Seville, Spain, who introduced the first two of their famous 'racehorse' quartet, *Brave Merchant* and *Dawn Merchant*. These ships (22,152gt, 180m, service speed 22.5 knots) had space for 130 commercial vehicles with passenger accommodation for 250 in 114 cabins.

In October 1999, Norse Irish Ferries was acquired by Cenargo for £30 million and their operations merged with those of Merchant Ferries and Belfast Freight Ferries, finally

In 1999 Merchant Ferries introduced the first of their famous 'racehorse' quartet, B*rave Merchant* and *Dawn Merchant* (pictured) to their new Liverpool-Dublin route. *(Gordon Hislip)*

becoming in February 2001. On 17th June 2002, the Twelve Quays river berth for ro-ro ferries on the Birkenhead side of the Mersey was opened, and with vessels no longer having to pass through Liverpool's enclosed docks system, the crossing time was greatly improved. Unfortunately, the parent company hit hard times, and had in 2003 to file for bankruptcy in the United States courts. Noting that the ferry company was still in a reasonably sound shape, the administrators restructured Cenargo thereby allowing Norse Merchant Ferries to have its debits significantly reduced.

In July 2005, a new *Lagan Viking* arrived at Belfast from her Italian builders with sister vessel, *Mersey Viking* following in the November. Both ships were upgrades of the previous two vessels which were then renamed *Liverpool Viking* and *Dublin Viking* respectively and transferred to replace the *Brave Merchant* and *Dawn Merchant* (sold to Spanish interests) on the Liverpool-Dublin service. The new *Lagan* and *Mersey Vikings* were improved versions of the previous ships each measuring 25,500gt and with a faster service speed of 23 knots. Passenger and cabin accommodation were for 980/480 persons respectively, with garage space for 160 cars as well as 160 trailers.

Just before the arrival of the two new ships, Maersk, the parent company of Norfolk Line, announced its intention to acquire Norse Merchant Ferries along with its relatively modern tonnage. Maersk needed the formal approval of both the UK and Irish competition commissions before they could conclude the deal. However, just a few years down the road in May 2009, Maersk announced it was planning to sell off Norfolk Line and other non-core activities and concentrate on its world-wide container services. The ferry services were eventually taken over by DFDS Seaways as from July 2010, with the vessels being rebranded in DFDS colours. The four ro-pax vessels on the Birkenhead-Belfast/Dublin routes were renamed with the 'Seaways' suffix replacing the 'Viking' nomenclature, i.e. *Lagan Viking* becoming *Lagan Seaways*.

This new venture was not to last very long as in December 2010, after losses of £30m, the Belfast side of DFDS' Irish Sea operations from Birkenhead and Heysham were suddenly sold to Stena Line. The two ro-ro vessels *Hibernia Seaways* and *Scotia Seaways* and the chartered ro-pax vessels *Lagan Seaways* and *Mersey Seaways* were included in the sale. DFDS' Birkenhead to Dublin and Heysham to Dublin services

were also closed at the end of January 2011 with no buyers in the offing.

The closure of the DFDS Seaways' Birkenhead-Dublin route marked the last foot-passenger crossing on the Liverpool route as rival operators P&O (Irish Sea) and Seatruck Ferries cater only for freight and cars/motorised homes. The *Liverpool Seaways* would find further employment in the DFDS fleet on their Baltic services, whilst the *Dublin Seaways* was sold to the Stena subsidiary Stena North Sea Ltd and renamed *Stena Feronia*. Since then she has seen service on charter to DFDS Seaways in the Baltic as well as returning to the Irish Sea to relieve during the refit periods. In 2015, she was sold to Strait Shipping, Wellington, New Zealand, renamed *Strait Feronia* and is currently deployed on their Bluebridge service between Picton and Wellington.

## Stena take over

Stena's purchase price for the two routes and four ships, *Hibernia Seaways* and *Scotia Seaways* (owned) and *Lagan Seaways* and *Mersey Seaways* (chartered) was said to be around £40m. Whilst it was referred to the UK or Irish Competition Commissions both agreed that the sale should be allowed to proceed. During the immediate period after the takeover the *Stena Lagan, Stena Hibernia* and *Stena Scotia,* as they were now renamed, continued to wear their blue hulled DFDS liveries with Stena funnel markings. The *Stena Mersey*, however, remained as delivered, in her original Norse Merchant red hull colours dating from 2005.

With both the *Stena Mersey* and *Stena Lagan* in need of refits and refurbishment and this began in stages in early 2012, when the ships visited Harland & Wolff in turn with Seatruck's *Clipper Pennant* providing freight cover. Each received the full Stena Line livery and branding on their hulls, much improving their outward appearance. Internally each underwent a £2.0m upgrade designed by Swedish company Figura to bring some of the rather spartan areas up to Stena Line standards. Much of this work was done whilst the ships were in service, but however, being on charter there was always a limit to that which the owners (Meridian Shipping) would authorise. The rebranded "Stena Metropolitan Bar and Restaurant' areas received new seating and carpeting, and the reclining seat areas were revamped into 'Stena Plus' lounges. Cabin and

The *Mersey Viking* of 2006 was a larger and improved version of her predecessor. She kept her red hull until 2012 when, now the *Stena Mersey*, she was given a complete makeover by Stena. *(Gordon Hislip)*

The *Lagan Seaways* in full DFDS livery which lasted less than a year as Stena Line took over the service in 2011. *(Gordon Hislip)*

The *Lagan Seaways* temporarily retained her DFDS blue hull and name prior to undergoing a major overhaul and repainting into the full Stena line livery. *(Gordon Hislip)*

Looking far better in full Stena livery, the *Stena Mersey* sets out along Belfast Lough for Birkenhead. *(Matt Davies)*

Observed at Birkenhead, the *Stena Forecaster* increased freight capacity on the Belfast-Birkenhead route, later being replaced by sister vessel *Stena Forerunner. (Matt Davies)*

corridor floors were at last carpeted, replacing the rather drab Formica tiled flooring.

Always prepared to do the unexpected, in late April 2012 Stena Line announced that they had purchased both ships, a typically shrewd move in that it would now give them the opportunity to upgrade and properly 'Stenarise' (if there is such a word) these basically excellent vessels throughout. In early January 2013 work began on refurbishing the remaining passenger areas of both vessels. The 'Barista Coffee Bar' was further enlarged and the children's play area (branded as 'Curious George' as per the rest of the fleet) now had X-Box game consoles to add to the entertainment, whilst Plasma TV screens were installed in the newly created Living Room lounge along with free Wi-Fi throughout. Perhaps the biggest change has come in the cabin accommodation which has always been rather basic. New Standard Class, Family Class and Comfort Class Cabins have been installed, all with fresh interiors and fittings, whilst the more superior Family and

The covering of snow on Belfast's Black Mountain makes a fine backdrop as the *Stena Lagan* slowly passes the *Stena Edda* on her morning sailing to Birkenhead. *(Gordon Hislip)*

Comfort Class cabins come complete with TV, tea and coffee making facilities, fridge with and complimentary soft drinks. Comfort Class also includes bathroom accessories, luxury linen and bathrobes!

Resulting from all these upgrades, passenger capacity was downsized to 720 though cabin accommodation remained at 480 berths. There is no doubt that these vessels are in their best condition ever and in consequence have been instrumental in boosting the fortunes of this important route.

In August 2018, freight capacity on the Birkenhead-Belfast route was increased by the arrival of the *Stena Forerunner* one of the versatile Stena 4-Runner Mark II class vessel. She was built at the Dalian Shipyard in China in 2003 and measures 24,688gt, 195m in length with a service speed of 22.5 knots. Her 3,000 lane metres for freight means that she could accommodate up to 200 trailers. In February 2019, she was returned to the Harwich-Europoort freight service and replaced by sister vessel *Stena Forecaster*, which, as a consequence of Covid-19 reducing freight demands, was stood down in May 2020

The introduction of the E-Flexer, *Stena Edda,* in January 2020 and the *Stena Embla* in 2021 is testament to how far the route has evolved in recent years thanks to Stena's efforts with the *Stena Lagan and Stena Mersey.*

Their future within the company appears to be assured as contracts were signed in September 2019 with Turkish shipyard SEDEF Shipbuilding Inc. for the lengthening and rebuilding of both the *Stena Mersey and Stena Lagan.* Stena RoRo are very adept at managing vessel conversion projects, which will give the vessels a similar capacity to the new . By extending them by 36 metres to 222.6 metres in length this will increase their freight capacity to 2,875 lane metres (190 trailers), and the dedicated car deck capacity to 280. Whilst Stena have currently limited passenger numbers to 720 it is expected that this will revert to the original 980 passenger figure, with cabin accommodation markedly up from 120 to 194 cabins.

Of greater significance, the ships will have twin level drive-through loading capabilities, NAOS Ship & Boat Design, the original designers of the ships being involved in the conversion work. At the stern the current lifting mechanism for the ramp will be replaced with a hydraulic solution.

Once the *Stena Edda* had settled in on her Irish Sea route,

With the County Antrim coastline well to the fore the *Stena Edda* is seen approaching Belfast Lough at the end of her crossing from Birkenhead. *(Stena Line)*

the *Stena Lagan* left for Turkey, arriving at Tuzla, near Istanbul on 31st March, with the conversion work expected to take around four months to complete. However, COVID-19 issues have meant her conversion work has had to be delayed; it is not clear when the project will begin. Stena have yet to confirm the ship's future deployment, somewhere in the Baltic being the most likely possibility, but one should never be surprised!

## The Stena Edda is delivered early

The *Stena Edda* was the second of Stena Line's newest generation of E-Flexer ships to be built at the China Merchants Jinling Shipyard (previously known as AVIC Weihai Shipyard Co., Ltd), Shandong Province in China. Naming her *Edda* is in keeping with the E-Flexer theme chosen to reflect main goals of the design, namely efficiency and flexibility, and is an Old Norse term applied to the medieval literary works known as Prose Edda or Poetic Edda which date from the 13th century.

The name of her running mate, *Stena Embla,* which will be in service in Spring 2021, also comes from Norse mythology. Ask and Embla are male and female respectively and said to be the first two humans created by the gods. The pair are mentioned in both the Poetic Edda and in the Prose Edda.

The construction of the *Stena Edda* took two years and one month from the time that the first pieces of steel were cut to being delivered to Stena Line, some five days ahead of schedule on 15th January 2020. The *Stena Edda* left Weihai for the first leg of her delivery voyage on 22nd January, making several stops including Singapore where the vessel took on sufficient bunkers to get to Europe. After a final stop at Algeciras she headed for Belfast.

Arriving in Belfast Lough late on 25th February, the *Stena Edda* anchored off Groomsport until the following morning. At first light, escorted by a flotilla of boats, she made her way to Belfast's Victoria Terminal 2 (VT2) for berthing trials, in doing so becoming the first ferry to visit the rebuilt berth where a new access ramp had been built specifically to accommodate the E-Flexer.

Like her sister *Stena Estrid*, the 41,671 gross tonnage new ship will accommodate up to 1,000 passengers, 120 cars on a dedicated car deck and with 3,100 lane metres on the vehicle decks there is space for up to 210 lorries. Over the past months the infrastructure at both ports has been improved with double-deck ramps to accommodate the 215m long ferry, aimed at faster loading and unloading for both passengers and vehicles. The works at Belfast were quite significant with the layout at the Belfast VT2 being redesigned to improve traffic flow.

By 28th February she had completed her berthing trials not just at Belfast VT2, but also at Stena's Loch Ryan Port at Cairnryan (to check her flexibility) and at her Twelve Quays South berth at Birkenhead. She remained at Birkenhead for crew training and to complete all statutory safety drills. At the same time contractors were making some final adjustments around the passenger accommodation.

On 9th March 2020, the *Stena Edda* made her maiden commercial voyage with Captain Krzysztof (Kris) Gadomski in command on the 21.30 departure from Birkenhead, replacing the *Stena Lagan* on the service. The ship has been very warmly received on both side of the Irish Sea and with her two sisters, *Stena Estrid* (Holyhead-Dublin) and *Stena Embla* (floated out 15th November 2019) arriving in Spring 2021, each costing over £150m, they represent a massive investment by Stena Line in enhancing ferry travel across the Irish Sea. These superb ships will surely repay dividends.

A tranquil view across the docks at Belfast with the *Stena Edda* taking centre stage. *(Stena Line)*

SIX

# North Channel Stranraer/Cairnryan – Larne/Belfast

## The Princess Steamships

**O**f the established crossings of the Irish Sea, the North Channel is the more steeped in history with records going as far back as 1662. The railways didn't arrive until two centuries later with the opening of the Portpatrick Railway from Castle Douglas to Stranraer in 1861, and shortly afterwards the Glasgow and Stranraer Steam Packet Company began running a ferry service from the latter town to Belfast. Within five years the Caledonian Railway Company, in conjunction with the London & North Western Railway (LNWR), had taken over the operation. When the Larne and Stranraer Company established their own service between the two ports in 1872, initially using the *Princess Louise,* this set a pattern for the future as the 'Princess' nomenclature itself would continue for more than a century with the *Galloway Princess* in 1980 being the last ship to be so named.

The sinking of the diesel powered vehicle ferry *Princess Victoria* on 31st January 1953 in a storm with 113 lives lost had left the powers that be on the North Channel in a state of shock, as this had been a vessel far ahead of its time. Her low stern gates were damaged in heavy seas and this allowed

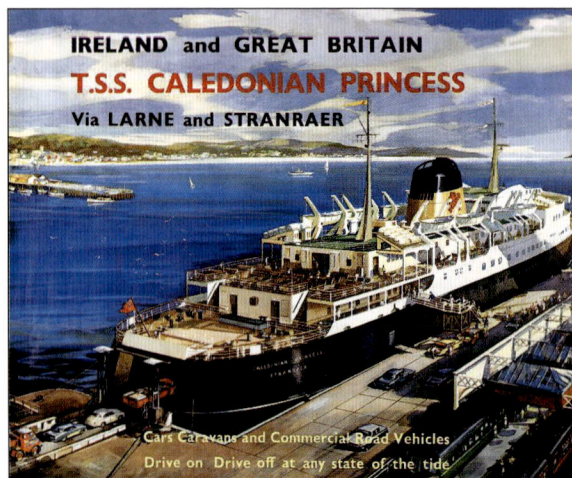

IRELAND and GREAT BRITAIN
T.S.S. CALEDONIAN PRINCESS
Via LARNE and STRANRAER

Cars Caravans and Commercial Road Vehicles
Drive on Drive off at any state of the tide

water to pour onto the car deck. Worse still the car deck freeing ports were far too small to drain any water away quickly. It would not be until 1957 that the British Transport Commission (BTC) would give approval for the construction of a new ship for the route and would be a further four years before the ship entered service in December 1961.

Operating under the aegis of the Caledonian Steam Packet Company (Irish Services Limited) the *Caledonian Princess* was another turbine steamship and not diesel driven which, in reality, was a retrograde step, with the ship subsequently having a relatively short 20 year service life. She measured 3,630gt, 108m in length and had a service speed of 19 knots. Advertised as an 'all-in-one' two-class ship with a passenger certificate for 1,400 passengers and berths for up to 176 persons, albeit these were all below the car deck. Her garage capacity was for 103 cars, with space for 29 small trailers, though any lorry over 22 feet would have to be backed on, which meant that loading could be a slow process. In a hangover from the past, lairage was provided for up to 70 cattle. More importantly, given the previous history on the route, great play was made about her having a watertight door

The turbine steamship *Caledonian Princess* (1961) captured at full speed in the late 1960's. She saw service on all the Sealink Irish Sea routes as well as those to the Channel Islands, before bowing out at Dover in September 1981. *(Ferry Publications Library)*

Chartered for the Stranraer-Larne service in 1966, *Stena Nordica* was the first drive-through ferry to operate for the British Railways Board. *(Ferry Publications Library)*

fitted at the stern. Whatever her shortcomings she was in the short-term a success with the public, proudly displaying her Scottish roots with a red lion rampant on her yellow funnel, before losing it in 1966 in favour of the new and iconic British Rail double arrow logo. Each year she made a working profit and by 1967 she had increased passenger carryings threefold to over 500,000 and cars fivefold to 100,00.

## Dieselisation

With another new ship planned to come into service for 1967 (*Antrim Princess*) the management had in January 1966 chartered the Swedish registered *Stena Nordica,* almost new, built in 1965. Relatively diminutive, the diesel-powered *Stena Nordica* was the first drive-through ferry to operate for a British Rail subsidiary, who up to then were still continuing to build stern loading turbine steamships. Despite her small size (and no stabilisers) she could accommodate nearly 1,000

Possibly lacking the grace of the *Caledonian Princess* in 1967 the highly successful *Antrim Princess* was British Rail's first drive through ferry, her fireman's helmet funnel becoming an icon in design. *(Ferry Publications Library)*

passengers and more importantly carry no less than 28 lorries or 120 cars on her vehicle deck. In essence the *Stena Nordica* was a stop-gap measure but stayed on until 1971 when the *Ailsa Princess* joined the *Antrim*.

The *Antrim Princess* was built by Hawthorn Leslie & Co. at Hebburn-on-Tyne in 1967 and looked far more up to date as British Rail's first seagoing ship to be fitted with a bow door as well as being diesel-powered. Her iconic fireman's helmet funnel became synonymous with British Rail and later Sealink ro-ro passenger ferries. She measured 3,360gt, was 112m in length, and had a service speed of 19 knots. Able to accommodate up to 170 cars and/or 28 lorries, her passenger certificate was for 1,200 persons. She initially retained the two-class structure and whilst internally her furnishings were of a high standard, she somehow lacked the panache of her predecessor, the *Caledonian Princess,* being built more with the needs of motorists and truckers in mind than of classic travellers.

Approaching the berth at Stranraer with bow visor raised, the ro-ro freighter *Ulidia* served from 1974 until the arrival of the *Galloway Princess* in 1980. *(Jim McIntyre)*

The Italian-built Stranraer-Larne ferry *Ailsa Princess* (1971), was a near sister to the *Antrim Princess*, complete with its own unique version of the BR funnel logo. She is seen with bow visor raised approaching her berth at Stranraer in May 1980. *(Tony Garner)*

Fleetmate *Antrim Princess* cautiously approaches the berth at Stranraer. *(Ferry Publications Library)*

The *Antrim Princess* served the route very effectively but managed to hit the news headlines on 9th December 1983 when she lost power following an engine room fire shortly after leaving Larne for Stranraer. With his vessel left powerless in severe gale conditions the Master issued a distress call and within 15 minutes helicopters from the RAF at Aldergrove (near Belfast) and naval Sea Kings from Prestwick were on the scene. In an amazing rescue in which eight helicopters were involved, the pilots and crewmen showing incredible skill and bravery, they airlifted all 108 passengers and 20 crew members to safety.

The Master, Captain Cree, and 32 officers and crew remained onboard, eventually the *Antrim's* anchors held and she was able to ride out the storm. It might be apocryphal, but when Captain Cree returned to Stranraer and attended his local church, the first hymn was reported to be 'Will your anchors hold through the storms of life'.

Constructed in Austria as *Stena Topper* in 1977, with hull and superstructure separately floated down the Danube to Galatz for welding together and Constanța for fitting out, the *Darnia* also had stabilisers fitted prior to entering service on the Stranraer-Larne route. *(Ferry Publications Library)*

The *Antrim Princess'* success on the Stranraer-Larne crossing served to increase the pressure on British Rail Board (BRB) bosses in London of the need for another ship. In July 1969 an order was placed with Cantiere Naval, Breda, Venice for a near sistership to the 'Antrim'. This decision raised a hue and cry with those who felt that British taxpayer's money shouldn't be spent outside of the country. BRB stuck to their guns saying that the decision was based on both delivery date and price, something that at the time was not one of UK shipyards' greatest assets.

In the following year work started on infrastructure improvements at Stranraer, including a new car ramp which managed to sink just a week after its opening in March 1971, following a mechanical problem. With the *Stena Nordica's* charter finally finishing at the end of that month and the *Ailsa Princess* not due into service until July, ASN's *Bardic Ferry* was chartered in before being replaced in early June by the brand new 1,599gt, 106m, Norwegian built ro-ro freight ferry *Dalriada* (1,599gt) from Stena Ab with a vehicle capacity for up to 35 lorries.

The arrival at Stranraer by the *St David* on 5th October 1985, saw the *Antrim Princess* transferred to the Isle of Man Steam Packet Company following their merger with Sealink, later being renamed *Tynwald*. By 1990 her days were

In February 1982 the *Darnia* was sent to Immingham to have her superstructure extended; she could now accommodate 400 passengers. *(Ferry Publications Library)*

A fine aerial view of the *Darnia* in Sealink British Ferries livery, her twin vehicle decks are being used to full capacity. *(Ferry Publications Library)*

numbered and after completing her final sailing on 18th February 1990 she was sold to Italy's Lauro Line and renamed *Lauro Express* running from Naples to Sicily and Tunisia.

The *Ailsa Princess* took up her services from Stranraer on 7th July 1971, similar in size to the *Antrim,* internally she differed very little in layout and continued with the tradition of being a two class ship. Externally, it was her funnel that caused most comment with the two horizontal lines of the BR logo carried right around the funnel. With full hanging decks above the main vehicle deck she could now accommodate up to 200 cars. For nearly two decades she would give excellent service but following the delivery of the *Galloway Princess* in 1980, the *Ailsa Princess* spent a peripatetic life on various Sealink routes. In 1985 she was moved to Weymouth for Channel Islands services and renamed *Earl Harold.* In November 1989 after spending the summer on charter to B&I for their Pembroke Dock-Rosslare service she was sold to Aktoploiki Maritime in Greece and renamed *Dimitra.*

With freight continuing to increase, in 1974 Sealink took advantage of purchasing the *Dalriada's* sister vessel, *Stena Carrier* (1,599gt), from Stena Ab, renaming her *Ulidia.* The *Dalriada* would remain in service on the North Channel route until August 1978, the *Ulidia* leaving two years later in 1980 after the new *Galloway Princess* had entered service.

In 1977, Sealink turned once more to Stena Ab for a further freighter, this was the *Stena Topper*, recently part constructed at Österreichische Sciffswerften AG, Korneuburg, Austria. From there she had been floated down the River Danube (hull and superstructure separately) to Galatz (Romania) to be welded together before being towed to Constanţa for final fitting out. Renamed *Darnia,* she was larger and longer than her consorts at 2,807gt and being a double-deck ferry was able to accommodate up to 75 trailers. Most importantly, she had stabilisers fitted before entering service at Harland & Wolff, Belfast making her a far more versatile ferry. Having impressed on the route, in 1982 she was sent to Immingham, Humberside, to have an accommodation block installed for 412 persons thus enabling her to carry passengers and cars as well as freight. She would remain on the Stranraer-Larne service until late 1990 when as part of Stena Line's reorganisation she was sold to Nordström & Thulin Ab, Stockholm mainly for Baltic Sea services as the *Nord Neptunus*, though from January 1991 until March 1993 she was on charter for Sally Line on their Dunkirk-Ramsgate service.

Above: A wonderful overhead image of the *Galloway Princess*, in her new Sealink British Ferries livery on yet another crossing to Larne. *(Ferry Publications Library)*

Top right: The *St David* arrives at Larne on late afternoon sailing from Scotland. *(Miles Cowsill)*

Middle right: With Stena Sealink Line branding on her hull, the renamed *Stena Caledonia* (ex *St David*) approaches her berth at Stranraer. *(Miles Cowsill)*

Right: Transferred from the Dover-Calais short-sea route, a smart-looking *Stena Antrim* (ex *St Christopher*) is observed at Stranraer. *(Miles Cowsill)*

Another view of the *Stena Caledonia*, this time at Larne. She was the last of the 'Saint'class to be built and after a rather peripatetic early career found her niche on the North Channel. *(Miles Cowsill)*

The lead ship of the 'Saint' class, the *Stena Galloway* (ex *Galloway Princess*) entering the buoyed channel off Larne. *(Miles Cowsill)*

Later, as the *Neptunia* from February 2000 through to June 2001 she was on the Boulogne-Folkestone route for Falcon Seafreight.

## A Final Princess

Coinciding with the *Darnia's* arrival in 1977 big changes were already afoot at Stranraer with the announcement that a new purpose-built ship was to be constructed at Harland & Wolff, Belfast, capable of carrying 600 (later raised to 1,000) passengers, 300 cars and/or 60 lorries. The ship, to be named *Galloway Princess*, was the first in a series of four which became known as the 'Saint' class as the other three all had that prefix. Designed by Tony Rogan and Don Ripley, Sealink's highly respected naval architects, they had to have the capability to be able to operate out of any port at all states of the tide whether or not they had single deck or double deck loading facilities. They achieved this by an ingenious series of

A splendid image of the *Stena Caledonia* leaving Larne on another crossing to Stranraer. *(Miles Cowsill)*

shortened ramps between the decks, an arrangement which later became the industry norm.

The *Galloway Princess'* entry into service was some ten months later than planned so it wasn't until 1st May 1980 that she made her maiden voyage, replacing the *Darnia*. At the same time the *Ulidia* was also deemed surplus and sent to Newhaven for lay-up and sale. At 6,268gt (remeasured as 12,711gt in 1985) and 128m in length, the *Galloway Princess* was far larger than anything so far seen on the North Channel route. Her service speed was a modest 18.5 knots, enough for the route, and having a bulbous bow she achieved a significant economy in power needs. On the downside her bow thrusts were slightly underpowered which called for careful ship handling in adverse weather conditions. Despite the usual gremlins that beset any new vessel, the *Galloway Princess,* settled down well on the route and became a very popular ship much loved by both public and crew alike.

In January 1986 the *St David* arrived at Stranraer, effectively replacing both the *Antrim Princess* and *Ailsa Princess,* to serve the alongside the *Galloway Princess* and *Darnia.* The last of the quartet of 'Saint' class vessels the *St David's (1981)* early career had been rather nomadic, originally earmarked for the Fishguard-Rosslare route but actually beginning her service life at Holyhead. During 1983 she saw periods of service on the Dover-Calais and Stranraer-Larne routes whilst in 1984 she undertook a spell on the Harwich-Hoek van Holland link. In 1985, she returned to Dover for Sealink British Ferries' ill-conceived service to Ostend which closed at the end of that year.

After Sealink British Ferries' six-year proprietorship came to an end in 1990, with Stena Line as the new owners, the fleet all received 'Stena' prefixes, the *Galloway Princess* being renamed as the *Stena Galloway,* thus becoming 'The Last Princess'. The *St David* was now the *Stena Caledonia,* a name which better reflected her routing. The *Darnia* was withdrawn and in her place came another of the 'Saint' class vessels, the *Stena Antrim,* the former *St Christopher.*

In November 1995, Stena Line closed their operations to Larne opening instead a new terminal at Belfast. This meant a longer journey time and revised timetables, but gradually traffic figures began to improve as hauliers took advantage of the superior road networks around Belfast to the rest of Northern Ireland.

123

It is interesting to compare the stern layout of the *Stena Antrim* viewed at Stranraer with that of the *Stena Caledonia* (opposite). Her aft superstructure was extended to increase passenger capacity on the Dover-Calais service when she was the *St Christopher*. *(Miles Cowsill)*

:A gamechanger! The introduction of the HSS *Stena Voyager* brought a fresh dimension to travel and a new port in Belfast. *(Miles Cowsill)*

A portent of things past or things to come? A warning sign at Stranraer, the HSS was soon required to slow down even more in Loch Ryan. *(Miles Cowsill)*

## High Speed Voyager

Never afraid to be innovative and bold, Stena Line confirmed that the second HSS craft would be on the North Channel, which meant major infrastructure changes at both Stranraer and Belfast. The *Stena Voyager* actually entered service quite soon after the *Stena Explorer* on 21st July 1996. The *Stena Antrim,* in temporary lay-up at Belfast, was quickly re-activated as the *Stena Voyager* was experiencing timetabling difficulties owing to longer passage times than expected. Her original 85-minute timetable had to be extended owing to speed restrictions in both Loch Ryan and Belfast Lough.

The *Stena Antrim* was later that year transferred to the Newhaven-Dieppe route to join her original running mate the *Stena Cambria* (ex *St Anselm*). Withdrawn from service in June 1998, she was sold to Lignes Maritimes du Detroit SA Casablanca, Morocco and renamed *Ibn Batouta.* She is still in service today, and sports a garish yellow hull as their *European Star* for services out of Brindisi.

Whilst the *Stena Voyager* was the designated HSS vessel for the Stranraer-Belfast service, she did occasionally cover for her sister ships when they became unavailable. In March 1997 she operated between Holyhead and Dun Laoghaire while the *Stena Explorer* received her first annual overhaul. In 1998, she spent over two months from 22nd January until the 4th April covering on the Hoek van Holland service after the *Stena Discovery* suffered damaged to her bow in rough weather. She returned to Belfast to pick up her service again as from 28th April.

The *Stena Caledonia* acted as the main freight support vessel the HSS, reverting to passenger mode as and when required. She had an interesting diversion in July 1998 when she was chartered to convey support vehicles between Cork and Roscoff for the Tour de France which had been visiting Ireland that year. In February 2000, in order to comply with the latest SOLAS regulations, the *Stena Caledonia* was sent to Birkenhead for an extended refit. The work included the addition of a duck-tail sponson to aid stability and reduce wash when sailing along Belfast Lough, as well as replacing her bow rudder with a bulbous bow.

In February 2002, the *Stena Galloway* was withdrawn and sold to the International Maritime Transport Corporation (IMTC), Casablanca, Morocco. Renamed *Le Rif* she saw service

Manoeuvring off Stranraer, the *Stena Caledonia* is seen in her final Stena Line livery. She remained in Stena service until November 2011 and today is the Port Link for an Indonesian company. *(Miles Cowsill)*

The *SeaFrance Manet* (1984), seen at Calais, was formerly the *Stena Parisien* and *Champs Elysees*. In 2009 Stena purchased the ship, renaming her *Stena Navigator*. (Miles Cowsill)

Looking absolutely resplendent in the full Stena Line livery, the well-travelled *Stena Navigator* is photographed bow-in at Stranraer. (Gordon Hislip)

on the Algerciras-Tangiers crossing, though at times it was somewhat intermittent. By 2014, she was in long-term lay-up but in a surprise move, after much legal argument, was acquired in 2019 by Africa Morocco Link and reactivated as their *Morocco Sun* for services between Algeciras and Tanger Med, a new port established about 40km east of Tangiers.

The *Stena Caledonia* continued on her Stranraer-Belfast service as scheduled, and each June between 2007 and 2009 she would be chartered out to Isle of Man Steam Packet on services between Douglas and Heysham/Belfast to help clear traffic associated with the TT races.

Overall, the *Stena Voyager* performed very reliably with relatively few incidents though in October 2007 a fire was discovered onboard in one of the *Stena Voyager's* engine rooms. The 601 passengers on board were issued with life jackets as the 'Voyager' made her way safely back to Belfast. The fire was extinguished by the onboard automatic systems in less than an hour and no one was injured, with the craft swiftly inspected and repaired at Belfast.

A potentially very dangerous incident occurred on 28th January 2009, the driver of an articulated HGV lorry carrying sulphite powder forgot to apply the handbrakes. As the HSS accelerated along Loch Ryan the vehicle broke free of its lashings, crashing through the No 1 stern door coming to rest with half of it hanging over the back of the craft. The HSS turned back for Stranraer, with the 156 passengers and 33 crew on board having a long wait until they could disembark. Eventually a mobile crane managed to lift the vehicle off to safety and the craft could berth properly.

**Enter the Navigator**

On July 8th 2009, Stena Line announced that they had acquired the *Seafrance Manet* for their Belfast-Stranraer operation. It seemed to be a strange choice for a ship that had been laid up for a year and said not to be in good condition. However, there was a shortage of suitable ferries available which could fit the berthing constraints in Stranraer whilst being large enough to be viable on their North Channel operation. If anyone could succeed in this respect it would be Stena with their ability to transform even the most unlikely ugly duckling into a beautiful swan.

After an overhaul and repaint at Dunkerque the *SeaFrance*

A classic image of the *Stena Navigator* at the entrance to Belfast Lough. Before entering service for Stena Line, she had a comprehensive refurbishment designed by Stena's house naval architects, Figura, receiving the prestigious Shippax award for the Best Ferry Conversion of 2009. *(Miles Cowsill)*

*Manet* arrived at Belfast on the 23rd September, in full Stena Line livery but with no name change. Dating from 1984 as the *Champs Elysees* for SNCF's Calais-Dover service, she became the *Stena Parisien* in 1992 for Stena Line on their Dieppe-Newhaven service, before returning to the Calais route in 1997 for SeaFrance. Measuring 15,093gt, 134m in length and with a service speed of 18.5 knots, the *Stena Navigator*, as she was to be renamed, had a passenger certificate for 1,800 persons and could accommodate either 330 cars or 46 lorries or a mixture of the two.

In order to bring her up to Stena Line standards, a comprehensive refurbishment designed by Stena's house naval architects, Figura, was carried out by Newry based MJM Marine alongside at Belfast, receiving the prestigious Shippax award for the Best Ferry Conversion of 2009.

The *Stena Navigator's* maiden voyage across the North Channel was on 12th November 2009 from Belfast and not surprisingly, given the length of time she had been laid-up, her early forays saw her experience several mechanical problems. Once the gremlins had been banished, she settled in becoming a very useful support vessel to the *Stena Voyager* and *Stena Caledonia*. Her presence on the Stranraer-Belfast service was always going to be short term as construction of a new terminal, Loch Ryan Port, just north of Cairnryan was about to get underway.

By now the *Stena Voyager's* operational costs had risen (largely down to swingeing increases in fuel) to the point of becoming 'unsustainable'. The final nail in the *Voyager's* coffin

128

Opposite page: The view from the more elevated bridge on the *Stena Caledonia* gave masters an excellent perspective over the vessel. The aft bridge was for intended for use when berthing at Holyhead. *(Miles Cowsill)*

Above: The lush pastures of Loch Ryan provide a perfect backdrop as the *Stena Caledonia* and *Stena Navigator* pass in close proximity, just outside of Stranraer. *(Miles Cowsill)*

was the decision by its owners to move its Scottish port of operation from Stranraer, which was now getting very rundown and in need of much fresh investment. The move would save 20 minutes on the journey which meant that modern conventional ships could now make the crossing almost as quickly as the HSS.

## A New Port

In March 2011, Stena Line announced that the *Stena Voyager*, *Stena Caledonia* and *Stena Navigator* were to be replaced in the autumn by the *Stena Superfast VII* and *Stena Superfast VIII*, chartered from Estonian ferry operator Tallink, and operate from the new Loch Ryan Port. Thus, 20th November 2011 marked the final day of ferry operations from Stranraer ending almost 150 years of operation, the displaced vessels all being laid up in Belfast awaiting sale.

The new 27 acre port at Loch Ryan at Old House Point, just north of Cairnryan, is an impressive facility making it one of the most modern in the UK. Its opening brought Stena Line's investment to revitalise the North Channel services to a massive £200m, including the new ships and infrastructure

'Making good time' seems to be an apt tag line, as the *Stena Caledonia* gets underway for another crossing to Belfast. *(Miles Cowsill)*

works at Belfast's Victoria Terminal 4 (VT4). At the opening ceremony on 25th November, Dan Sten Olsson, chairman of Stena Ab, commented that when Stena invests in infrastructure on this scale it is with a view of recouping the cost over the next half century. This in turn safeguards the ferry link between Scotland and Northern Ireland for the next generations to come. The port's geographical position has enabled the new ships to complete the crossing in 2 hours 15 minutes and be able to operate up to 12 sailings each day between Loch Ryan and Belfast. Within a year of opening and despite challenging economic conditions the new route had delivered a strong 9% increase in passenger numbers and a 60% increase in freight volumes.

The *Stena Navigator* remained laid up for nearly three months until mid-February 2012 when having been sold to Balaeria (Spain) she arrived at Santander for dry-docking. She re-emerged on the 9th of March in the full Balaeria livery and renamed *Daniya* for services between Denia and San Antonio to Palma or Barcelona. By November 2013 the ship had been moved by the company to the Algeciras-Cueta route and renamed *Poeta López Anglada*. In 2020, she was observed regularly operating between Algeciras and Tanger Med, a newly opened port roughly 40km east of Tangiers.

In May 2012 the *Stena Caledonia* was sold to Indonesia who subsequently renamed her *Port Link*, departing Belfast in the July. Not much more is known as to her movements but in June 2020 she was still in active service for the Indonesian company on their Merak-Bakauheni service.

As for the *Stena Voyager* she would remain at Belfast for nearly 17 months before in April 2013 being towed to the Öresundsvarvet Shipyard, Landskrona, Sweden, to be dismantled by Stena Line's sister company Stena Recycling Ab.

*A more comprehensive description of the HSS and the technology behind it is to be found in Chapter 4 - Innovative HSS.*

The old and the new meet up on a slightly murky day in November 2011 off the new Loch Ryan port. The *Stena Caledonia* was on one of her final sailings to Belfast with the *Stena Superfast VII* waiting to takeover. *(Miles Cowsill)*

## Stena Superfasts tear up the Channel

Stena Line were known to have been interested in Tallink's *Superfast VII* and *Superfast VIII* for a little while prior to 2011, as the Hanko (Finland) and Rostock (Germany) was reportedly losing money and the parent company was trying to restructure their debts. In March 2011 it was announced that Stena Line had agreed to charter both vessels for an initial three-year period which would later be extended until Autumn 2019.

The two ships were built for the Attica Group subsidiary, Superfast Ferries, by Howaldtswerke-Deutsche Werft in Kiel, Germany, who had an excellent reputation with regard to quality of work. Part of a series of four ships (*Superfasts VII-X*) built to the same design they were delivered in 2001/2. The *Superfast X* would see service for Stena Line on their Holyhead-Dublin service from 2015-2020 – see Chapter 3.

The ships measure 30,285gt, 203m in length and, as

The *Stena Navigator* is photographed in Loch Ryan on her last passenger voyage on the Stranraer service. *(Miles Cowsill)*

133

The *Stena Superfast VII* unloading coach traffic at the new Loch Ryan Port which nestles in a beautiful setting; a welcome change from the industrial landscapes in which many ports are located. *(Gordon Hislip)*

The *Stena Superfast VII* swings off her berth at Belfast in April 2013, having arrived from Loch Ryan Port. In the background, the HSS *Stena Voyager* is shortly to be towed to Sweden for scrapping, having spent 17 months up for sale. *(Gordon Hislip)*

designed, had an operating speed of 28.6 knots, though today a service speed of 22 knots is the norm. Being originally night-boats their passenger capacity was for just 717 passengers (the majority having cabins), whereas today operating on shorter routes this has now been raised to 1200 persons. Garage space is for either 660 cars or 110 lorries or a mix of the two. Renamed *Stena Superfast VII* and *Stena Superfast VIII* they were chartered to replace the HSS *Stena Voyager* and the two previous conventional ferries, *Stena Caledonia* and *Stena Navigator*, which had operated between Stranraer and Belfast.

Being designed as overnight ferries and now to be placed on a 2hr 15min Cairnryan (Loch Ryan Port) to Belfast an extensive conversion and refurbishment was needed to be undertaken. Overseen by Stena Ro-Ro collaboration with the eminent marine architects Knud E Hansen the work was undertaken at the Remontowa Shipyard in Gdansk, Poland, was rumoured to cost around £12m.

Structurally there was the need to be able to

*Stena Caledonia* and *Stena Navigator* laid up at Belfast awaiting new owners following the closure of Stranraer. *(Gordon Hislip)*

Outward bound from Loch Ryan Port, the *Stena Superfast VII* begins to pick up speed as she nears the open sea. Internally luxurious, she and her sistership claim to be the only ferries on the Irish Sea to offer a 'Pure Nordic Spa'. *(Miles Cowsill)*

The *Stena Superfast VIII* arrives off Milleur Point, at the northern end of Loch Ryan in bound from Belfast. From the heights above Loch Ryan, one can easily identify the ships as the uppermost deck on the *Stena Superfast VII* is painted blue, whilst on the *Stena Superfast VIII*, it is a sandy colour. *(Gordon Hislip)*

A rare meeting on the North Channel, the *Stena Superfast VIII* passes P&O's *European Seaway*, the latter is normally based at Dover but was covering for the refits of the regular vessels. *(Gordon Hislip)*

accommodate full height freight on both lorry decks so on the upper vehicle deck the free height was increased to over 5m in the centre four lanes. The ships can now to carry a total of 30 double-decked trailers of the type commonly used by supermarkets on the upper vehicle deck as and when required. Whilst there are also two car decks below the main vehicle deck (Decks 1 and 2) these are only used on the busiest sailings as normally most traffic can be accommodated on the two main vehicle decks.

Much of the original interior was revamped to designs provided by Figura with the outfitting work undertaken by Newry based MJM Marine. Much of Deck 7 is now taken up by the 'Taste Restaurant' (midships) and 'Met Bar' (forward), with a children's play area, a video game arcade, 'Stena Shopping' and 'Guest Services' occupy the remaining space. After a further refurbishment in 2018, the little used cinema on this deck was replaced by the 'Hygge Recline Lounge', which is a Danish term meaning, amongst other things, a feeling of slowing down and enjoying cosiness. Luxury indeed!

Deck 8 was originally purely for cabin accommodation but is now the upper passenger amenities deck. Here one can find the 'Truckers Lounge' (forward), whilst aft there is the 'Barista Coffee Bar' and 'Stena Plus' lounge and number separate other lounges to relax in. It wasn't a case just of removing the 128 cabin modules as new larger windows had to be installed to replace the small cabin ones first fitted.

Deck 9 is for crew use only, whilst on Deck 10 cabin suites are available for guests at an additional fee. Deck 10 also houses the 'Pure Nordic Spa', billed as the only spa on the Irish Sea. Viewed from the heights above Loch Ryan, one can easily detect identify which ship is which as the uppermost deck on the *Stena Superfast VII* is painted blue, whilst on her sistership, the *Stena Superfast VIII,* it is a sandy colour.

On the mechanical side, Stena installed new propellers with blades designed for better fuel consumption, the ships are still capable of over 25 knots if necessary. In addition, the vessels are able to operate at their service speed on just two of their four Wärtsilä-Sulzer 16-cylinder diesel engines. A third KaMeWa bow thruster was installed in order to improve their manoeuvrability in port. The new port at Loch Ryan has an automated mooring system installed which removes the need for traditional mooring lines to be used, though in practice the lines are still available if need be, with the whole operation controlled from the ship's bridge.

On the 31st December 2017, Stena subsidiary Stena North Sea Ltd. purchased to the two vessels from Tallink in a deal said to be around £110m. Once again Stena Line have made yet another shrewd investment, the ships are fit for purpose, traffic figures are booming, a testament to the business acumen and foresight of the company.

# SEVEN

# Flexible Future

## Matt Davies takes an on-board look at the new Stena E-Flexers

The entry into service of the *Stena Estrid* and the *Stena Edda* marks the culmination of six years of planning and construction of a new generation of efficient ro-pax ferries being built in numbers of the like never seen before. The pair, which represent the first two of nine E-Flexers being built (five currently intended to be operated by Stena directly), were ordered by parent Stena Ro-Ro in March 2016 from the AVIC Weihai Shipyard in China after more than two years of design work. They were initially part of a two-vessel order with an option for a further two vessels. This option was quickly taken up with Stena Ro-Ro announcing further options for

four more vessels and long-term charters with other operators; Brittany Ferries taking three E-Flexers for UK to Spain services and DFDS a vessel for Dover - Calais. Stena Ro-Ro has since negotiated options for a further three E-Flexers, potentially increasing the total build to eleven vessels. It was later confirmed that vessels eight and nine in the series would be 239 metre lengthened versions of the original 215 metre design. Where they will operate is not yet known, Holyhead-Dublin or Birkenhead-Belfast may be options as well as the Baltic. The Baltic routes between Karlskrona-Gdynia and Nynäshamn-Ventspils have been speculatively mentioned

The CMI Jinling Weihai Shipyard with **Stena Estrid** (left) prior to floating out with **Stena Edda** under construction (right). (CMI Jinling Weihai Shipyard)

The *Stena Edda* being floated out after her naming ceremony on 15th April 2019. *(CMI Jinling Weihai Shipyard)*

The Builders Plate on the *Stena Estrid*. *(Matt Davies)*

purely on the basis that their increased cabin capacity suggests deployment on an overnight service. The options for vessels ten and eleven have yet to be exercised as confirmed orders by Stena Ro-Ro.

In creating the Stena E-Flexer, Stena Ro-Ro set out to improve efficiency, environmental performance and operating flexibility, adopting the name E-Flexer, for which 'E' stands for efficiency. Vehicle decks are efficiently laid out with around 50% more volume available within the same space as similar dimension ro-pax ferries. The result is a high-capacity flexible vessel that can operate on long overnight voyages, day voyages or on intensive short sea crossings with quick port turnarounds utilising either double or single deck loading infrastructure as available. It is a vessel that is suitable for operation by both Stena Line and by other ferry operators through sale or charter. The E-Flexer hull is purposely strengthened for Ice Class 1C or 1A certification ensuring a capability for worldwide ferry operations including those in the Baltic.

The E-Flexer design also has what Stena refer to as 'Stenability' built into to it, so as to easily allow future modifications on a cost-efficient basis. Lengthening or inclusion of additional vehicle decks or mezzanine decks, modification of passenger areas to increase day facilities or cabin numbers, changes in fuel types or fitment of scrubbers

141

*Stena Estrid* and *Stena Edd*a under construction.

Top left: The navigation bridge of the *Stena Edda* which was constructed separately is seen prior to being lifted on board and connected with the superstructure.

Top right: The extensive scaffolding used during the hull construction of the *Stena Estrid*.

Above: The area that will become the *Stena Estrid*'s forward Stena Plus Lounge takes shape.

Middle right: The *Stena Estri*d's aft stairwell under construction.

Right: The forward superstructure prior to the navigation bridge being joined to the *Stena Edda*'s superstructure.

*(All photos by Philippe Holthof)*

A three quarter aft view of the *Stena Estrid* taken whilst under construction from dock floor of CMI Jinling Weihai Shipyard. *(Philippe Holthof)* 143

A bow view of the *Stena Estrid* whilst under construction. In the background is the *Stena Edda*. *(Philippe Holthof)*

can all easily be achieved. With the order for lengthened vessels and the chartered vessels being fitted out in different formats, e.g. the provision of additional cabins for Brittany Ferries and day ferry requirements for DFDS, 'Stenability' is already being proven.

Brittany Ferries have signed an agreement with Stena to receive three of the new ferries on long-term charters. All three vessels will be customised using Spanish architects to create a typically local feel related to the places from which they take their names. The first, *Galicia* which enters service in 2020 will be conventionally powered, whilst the second, *Salamanca* (due 2022), will be LNG powered for their long-haul services between Portsmouth/Plymouth and Bilbao/Santander. Whilst utilising them on the Portsmouth-Le Havre service has also been mentioned, this proposal could well be just to facilitate crew changes each week. The third ship *Santoña* (due 2023) will also be LNG, her deployment still has yet to be decided, but almost certainly she will be on the Spanish routes. Cabin capacity on these ships will be increased to around 300 (with a further 36 for lorry drivers) by using the space taken up by the motorists' dedicated car deck and extending the superstructure on Decks 7 and 8 further aft. In addition, both LNG vessels will have their heavy vehicle deck capacity reduced from 3,100 lane metres to 2,758 lane metres in order to accommodate the extra equipment needed for LNG operation, including fuel tanks.

DFDS's E-Flexer, to be named *Côte d'Opale,* will be modified in a different way in order to operate on the short-sea service between Calais and Dover as from 2021. For this she will have her bow and stern loading arrangements heavily adapted to ensure compatibility with the berths at Dover and Calais. A third bow thrust unit will be installed to aid berthing in adverse conditions. Whilst the 120 vehicle capacity car deck on Deck 7 will be retained, the ship will not have any passenger cabins owing to the short nature of the 90-minute crossing, that space being used for further passenger amenities. As a result, the *Côte d'Opale* will have a slightly different profile.

Although constructed in China, the Stena E-Flexer series were designed in Europe by Finnish Naval Architects Deltamarin in conjunction with Stena Ro-Ro and Stena's design team Stena Teknik, with interior design on all the vessels undertaken by the Swedish Company Figura

145

The *Stena Estrid* is tested at full speed in reverse whilst on sea trials in the Yellow Sea. *(CMI Jinling Weihai Shipyard)*

Arkitekter. The E-Flexers feature a great many European components including Caterpillar engines, Wärtsilä thrusters and auxiliary engines, MaK propellers and glazing from French manufacturer Saint-Gobain. In fact, over 60% of components are European. Deltamarin provided Stena with a comprehensive engineering, procurement, construction and management package which also included on site supervision supporting AVIC with the vessels' construction.

Stena believe the *Stena Estrid* and *Stena Edda* are the 'best in class' for fuel efficiency with a significantly lower emissions footprint per freight unit than any other Ro-Pax ferry of similar size. In total it is believed they will contribute some 25% less in $CO_2$ emissions. For now, both will operate on low sulphur fuel, but the design is 'gas ready' and can be

converted to operate on LNG or Methanol. In addition, the design is also able to accommodate scrubbers as well as catalytic converters, thus providing complete flexibility for the future. Brittany Ferries has already opted to use LNG for the second and third of their vessels which will have tanks incorporated into the hull on Deck 1. Stena, meanwhile, is exploring several alternatives including methanol and battery power across its ferry operation before making any long term decisions.

The E-Flexer design is powered by twin Caterpillar MaK 12 M43 C 126,000kW diesel engines driving two controllable pitch propellers via reduction gears which, coupled with a very efficient hull form, allows the vessel to achieve a 22 knot service speed without a third or fourth engine. Each engine

Following float out on 15th April 2019 the *Stena Edda* is seen being prepared for towing to the fitting out berth at CMI Jinling Weihai Shipyard. *(CMI Jinling Weihai Shipyard)*

The uppermost outside deck on the *Stena Estrid*. The funnel has been designed with a void space on either side to allow for the fitment of scrubbers. (*Matt Davies*)

Inside the navigation bridge on the *Stena Estrid*. (*Matt Davies*)

One of the two Caterpillar MaK 12 M43C Engines on board the *Stena Estrid*. Each is located within a separate engine room compartment. (*Matt Davies*)

drives a feathering controllable pitch propeller via a RENK gearbox. The engines can operate together or in isolation with the propeller of the unused engine feathered so it can freely spin and thus minimise drag. As a result, the E-Flexer can achieve 18 knots on a single engine. The hull is hydro-dynamically efficient and includes an optimised bow bulb and a wave minimising stern to ease passage through water. With two less engines on-board, not only is less fuel used but weight is reduced significantly providing further benefit. Consequently, even when running with conventional low-sulphur fuel oil the E-Flexers will burn 1,300 tones less fuel annually than existing ferries of similar capacity. Stena has extensive experience of operating vessels with only two engines with their Visentini ro-pax fleet and have found them to be highly efficient.

In keeping with Sweden being ranked as one of the most sustainable countries in the world and as a Swedish company, Stena has taken every effort to ensure the E-Flexer design has a reduced environmental footprint. WE-Drive permanent magnet shaft generators have been installed along with an electrical distribution system which enables power to be supplied at optimum efficiency across the vessel, including to its bow thrusters and when in port. Energy consumption is further reduced through the use of LED lighting together with solar film being applied to glazing in order to reduce the air conditioning and heating needs. In addition, anti-fouling hull paint containing a bio-repellent ingredient and bio-degradable lube oils are used for the propellers and other sea interfaces. Multi-fraction recycling facilities and a targeted reduction in single-use plastic on-board all further help improve the E-Flexer's environmental footprint.

Construction of first vessel, the *Stena Estrid,* took 27 months from the start of steel cutting on 26th August 2017, keel laying taking place on 2nd February 2018. The hull and superstructure were constructed using 304 blocks which were assembled in a building dock prior to float out on 20th February 2019. After fitting out, the *Stena Estrid* commenced sea trials on 5th September 2019 with further sessions during October. They were conducted jointly under the supervision of Stena Line, classification society DNV-GL and the UK Maritime and Coastguard Agency (MCA). The trials which saw the *Stena Estrid* achieve 22.8 knots were to ensure all of her systems were fully operational and performing in line with the

build specification and covered areas such as engine performance and fuel consumption, navigation and radio equipment, emergency systems, speed tests, manoeuvrability, engine and thruster tests, vibration and noise insulation and safety.

Following handover to Stena Line on 15th November 2019, the *Stena Estrid* departed Weihai on 22nd November 2019 bound for Holyhead under the command of Senior Master Mathew Lynch with a crew of 27. The 10,000-mile voyage involved crossing the South China and East China seas to Singapore, then the Malacca Straits to Galle, Sri Lanka, across the Indian Ocean to the Gulf of Aden and via the Suez Canal to the Mediterranean with a call at Algeciras. For the large part it was conducted at economical speed of 17 knots using just one of the twin Caterpillar MaK 12 M43 C engines. The vessel arrived at Dublin on 22nd December 2019 for berthing trials from where she proceeded overnight to Holyhead, arriving the next morning. On Monday 13th January, in stormy conditions, the *Stena Estrid* undertook her maiden sailing from Holyhead to Dublin. She makes two round trips each day on the 3 hours 15 minutes crossing departing Holyhead at 08:55 and 20:30 and Dublin at 14:50 and 02:15. The vessels offers a 50% increase in freight capacity over the *Stena Superfast X* which she has replaced.

Construction of the *Stena Edda* took 25 months with steel cutting commencing on 15th December 2017, the keel being laid on 15th June 2018 and float out taking place on 15th April 2019. Sea trials commenced on 10th December and were quickly accomplished along with vessel acceptance allowing Stena Line to take delivery on 15th January 2020. On 22nd January 2020, the *Stena Edda* set sail from Weihai under the command of Senior Master Neil Whittaker, following the same path as the *Stena Estrid* to Belfast where she arrived just over a month later on 25th January 2020. After conducting berthing trials in Belfast, Cairnryan and Birkenhead and completing crew training, storing and certification, the *Stena Edda* undertook her maiden voyage on the 8-hour crossing from Liverpool (Birkenhead) to Belfast on 9th March 2020, the celebrations on-shore including a countdown light show. To accommodate the *Stena Edda* and sister *Stena Embla* (which is expected in early 2021) new double deck loading ramps have been built at Birkenhead's Twelve Quays Terminal at a cost of £17 million and at the Belfast Harbour VT2 Terminal

*Stena Edda* being towed backwards to the fitting out berth in April 2019 at CMI Jinling Weihai Shipyard with *Stena Estrid* in background. *(CMI Jinling Weihai Shipyard)*

costing £15 million by Peel Ports and the Belfast Harbour Commissioners respectively. The pair each offer 40% more vehicle deck capacity and 30% more fuel efficiency than the two Visentini Ro-Pax *Stena Lagan* and *Stena Mersey* which they replace.

AVIC Weihai was taken over in July 2019 by another Chinese state-owned shipbuilder, China Merchants Jinling Shipbuilding, who had little experience in building passenger ferries. Consequently, the lead time on the initial E-Flexers was longer than for those now in build. AVIC had required the need for a modular cabin production facility at the yard from where 239 fully completed cabins were built by German Manufacturer Reinhold & Mahla for each vessel prior to being lifted on-board, fitted in place and connected into the ships electric, water and waste systems.

The on-board layout and facilities of the Stena *Estrid* and *Stena Edda,* each of which is 41,671gt and can carry 1,000 passengers, are identical. In total 3,100 lane metres for freight are available allowing 210 units to be carried. Meanwhile, the extended 240 metre version of the E-Flexer design will offer 3,600 lane metres and accommodation for 1,200 passengers. The majority of vehicles are housed on the two main 5.2-metre-high freight decks on Levels 3 and 5, which offer 1,320 and 1,435 lane metres respectively. The rear of this upper vehicle deck is open in order to provide a secure area for the carriage of hazardous loads. In addition, 345 lane metres are available in a 4.8 metre height lower hold forward of the engine room on Deck 1 with access by a fixed ramp covered by a hatch.

Although designed for quick and efficient drive through loading and unloading on twin levels with bow and stern doors, a bi-directional tilting ramp on the port side links Decks 3 and 5. This allows the E-Flexers to serve ports without double deck berths, albeit with an increase in turnaround time. On Deck 7 at the stern and reached by another bi-directional tilting ramp on the starboard side is the dedicated motorist car deck which can hold 120 cars and offers a direct walk-through access to the adjoining Guest Services reception area on the same level. On the Brittany Ferries vessels, the first of which is due for delivery in late Autumn this year, the upper deck car area is being fitted out as additional cabin accommodation and the passenger accommodation on Deck 8 above further extended over the open aft section of the car

The *Stena Estrid* is formerly handed over by CMI Jinling Weihai Shipyard to Stena Lina in a ceremony at the yard on 15th November 2019. *(CMI Jinling Weihai Shipyard)*

deck to provide further cabins.

The *Stena Edda* and *Stena Estrid* are amongst some of the first vessels meeting new international maritime regulations covering the safe return to port (SRtP) which requires vessels over 120 metres in length to be able to return to port in an emergency. The means is achieved through including segregating the engines into separate compartments, back up machinery, splitting cable routing and provision of a second bridge fitted with key navigational equipment for use in an emergency. Located at the base of the forward mast, this small emergency bridge can easily be identified by its windows. Enhancing safety, a large helideck is also included.

Passenger facilities on the *Stena Estrid* and the *Stena*

Stena Line Chairman Dan Sten Olsen at the handover of the *Stena Estrid*. *(Stena Line)*

The *Stena Edda* departs CMI Jinling Weihai Shipyard bound for the U.K. on 22nd January 2020. *(CMI Jinling Weihai Shipyard)*

The *Stena Edda* anchored in the Bay of Gibraltar on 21st February 2020 whilst undertaking bunkers in readiness for the final leg of her delivery 10,000-mile voyage to Belfast. *(Peter Ferrary)*

*Edda* are spread over three decks; Decks 7, 8 and 9 and have been purposely designed to be light and airy with large panoramic windows and feature a central atrium. Wi-Fi is available throughout both vessels. Deck 7 comprises the dedicated car deck aft with walk-through access to a central stairwell. Above on Decks 8 and 9 are two aft located blocks of accommodation totalling 684 berths within 175 cabins, each having an 'infotainment' television system. There are four types of cabins; 167 inside or outside four berth cabins, 2 disabled two berth cabins and 6 deluxe cabins which are located on Deck 9. The latter have two berths with a double bed, large bathroom and a fridge, plus an external door allowing direct access to the outside rear deck. Cabin corridors are brightly decorated with multi striped technicolour carpets with graphics of European cities.

Passengers boarding via the car deck are met with 'nice to see you' messages projected onto the floor in the stairwell and

153

in the Guest Services area which also houses a 'Barista Coffee Bar' counter. Kitted out with a mix of laminate and soothing grey carpeting and upholstery it has seating for 130. In the middle is a staircase leading upwards to the atrium area of the 'Sky Bar' above on Deck 8. Outside access is available either side to the sheltered port and starboard side promenades with an enclosed room off the latter having heated dog kennels.

Moving forward a walkway runs along the port side, with seating and toilets to port and the 'Outlet On-board' shop to starboard with, towards the bow, the ship's galleys and stores. Featuring a bright red and white minimalist décor with grey striped flooring, the shop includes dual purpose tills which can be rotated so they can be operated as self-scan tills as now found in supermarkets. Located forward at the end of the walking passage and covering the full width of the vessels is the 325 seat 'Taste' Restaurant with its bow views, finished with a mix of orange and blue seating areas mixed with light Scandinavian woods, laminate flooring and blue carpeting.

Completing the modern feel are large interactive digital LCD screen menus. Adjacent to the entrance to 'Taste' is a small enclosed glazed children's playroom, one of two 'Happy World' branded play areas on-board. The Happy World brand centres around 'Happy', a friendly porpoise, and features artwork rather reminiscent of Finding Nemo.

Above on Deck 8, starting at the bow and working back, is the large 'Stena Plus Premium Lounge' with views forward. It has seating for 140 and is furnished with grey patterned carpets and a mix of light and dark woods with grey and black seating contrasting with sections of blue. As is usual, passengers can help themselves to a range of hot and cold drinks and snacks with table service available for more substantial meals. Numerous interesting Swedish design objects including books, household items and ornaments are spread over the lounge on shelves and in glass cases. Adding to the interest are several soft 'sleeping bears' located on the floor.

The *Stena Estrid* arriving at Dublin. *(Gordon Hislip)*

A night time view of the atrium area of the Sky Bar on Deck 8. *(Matt Davies)*

155

Top left: **One of the two identical Movie Lounge's located on Deck 8.**

Top right: **The 325 seat self-service Taste Restaurant located forward on Deck 7.**

Above: **The 140 seat Stena Plus lounge located forward on Deck 8.**

Middle right: **The mid-ships Barrista Coffee Bar Lounge on Deck 7 which has seating for 130 and is located adjacent to Guest Services.**

Above: **The Truckers Restaurant on Deck 8 which can cater for 170 drivers.**

*(All photos Matt Davies)*

The aft stairwell which is of a minimalist design. (*Matt Davies*)

The walk through entrance to Guest Services from the car deck on Deck 7. (*Matt Davies*)

The cabin corridors feature colourful carpets and European City Graphics which include John Lennon in Liverpool.. (*Matt Davies*)

A four berth outside cabin. (*Matt Davies*)

The aft superstructure view from the car deck on Deck 7 with the bi-directional tilting ramp lowered to link with the upper vehicle deck down below. (*Matt Davies*)

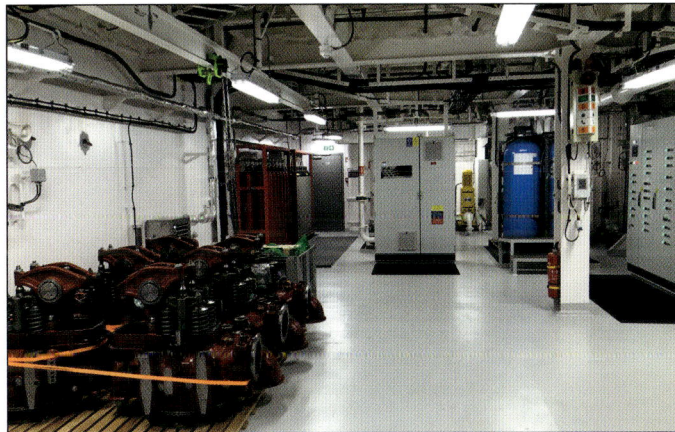

Top: A view of the upper vehicle deck on Deck 5 with the bi-directional tilting ramp which leads to and from the upper car deck on Deck 7. *(Matt Davies)*

Top right: The bi-directional vehicle ramp as seen from the dedicated car deck on Deck 7. *(Matt Davies)*

Above: The spacious electrical room on Deck 1. In the foreground are spare engine components. *(Matt Davies)*

Middle right: Looking across the spacious engine room console. *(Matt Davies)*

Right: An interesting view of the keel plating deep in the stern of the hull. *(Matt Davies)*

Tugs begin to manoeuvre Brittany Ferries' *Galicia* to her fitting out dock after being floated out on 11th September 2019. *(CMI Jinling Weihai Shipyard)*

DFDS' *Côte D'Opale* which was floated out on 22nd May 2020 is viewed at her fitting out berth. *(CMI Jinling Weihai Shipyard)*

Behind the 'Stena Plus Lounge' and accessed from the walkway offset to the port side of Deck 8 is the 'Hygge Premium Reclining Lounge'. Without windows in order to encourage guests to snooze away, it features grey carpets, dark wood and 32 sumptuous grey upholstered reclining chairs each with reading light and access to power points. Passenger wanting to access the 'Hygge' and 'Stena Plus' lounges and have not pre-booked can do so using a touch screen outside both entrances. On the port side of the walkway is the 'The Living Room' with an open seating area of blue upholstered sofas and fixed swivel seats with large LCD TV screens. On the other side of the walkway is interactive experience wall spread over four large LCD screens where passengers can play a quiz game. Moving aft behind the 'Hygge Lounge' on the starboard side is the 'Truckers Lounge' which features table seating for 170 in a mix of orange,

The *Stena Edda* at the Twelve Quays Terminal, Birkenhead having just arrived on 28th February from Weihai via Belfast and Cairnryan. After crew training and completion of all statutory safety drills she made her maiden commercial voyage on 9th March 2020. *(Matt Davies)*

A view across the Jinling Weihai Shipyard taken on 23rd May 2020. From left to right the *Galicia*, *Côte D'Opale* and *Stena Embla*, the latter being floated out on 15th November 2019. *(CMI Jinling Weihai Shipyard)*

maroons and browns along with a self-service food servery counter. Adjacent to this facility on the starboard side is a small video games area whilst on the port side is a further 'Happy World' play area.

Located mid-ships is the impressive 'Sky Bar' which runs the full width of the vessel and has a glass atrium ceiling extending through to Deck 9 above as a focal point. Featuring a mix of grey and brown upholstery, dark wood and metal finishes it has seating for 170 with an open staircase leading from the atrium down to the Guest Services lobby area below on Deck 7. There are several nice little touches including bronze angels sat on the ceiling lights in the atrium and two small metallic men statues each looking through a pair of binoculars.

Aft of the 'Sky Bar', and before the main stairwell on both the port and starboard sides, are two small 'Movie' lounges where films are shown for free. Symmetrically identical they are finished in greys with dark woods, more like lounges than cinemas. Each has three 65" screens with chairs scattered around them at angles in a way you would watch a movie at

home. Beyond is the aft stairwell and the lower of the two cabin blocks containing 88 cabins.

Finally, above on Deck 9 is the bridge, with behind it, the crew areas containing 63 cabins and a mess room for the crew of 73. It also houses a hospital bay, whilst further aft is the second of the two passenger cabin blocks with 87 cabins. Outside deck space on the vessels is plentiful and in addition to the wide and sheltered side promenades on Deck 7, there are balcony decks to the rear of Decks 8 and 9. Above on Deck 10 is a large open area which runs either side of the funnel to meet mid-ships by the atrium skylight.

With the E-Flexer, Stena has come up with a ferry that is not only modern and contemporary enough to give travellers a most pleasant high-quality voyage experience but one which is also incredibly efficient, flexible and future proof. Built in China with the best of European components and under Stena's expert supervision, Stena Ro-Ro have most certainly achieved high quality at a very good price. This Stena E-Flexer design is likely to be an incredibly successful series of vessels.

**Key Data – Stena Estrid, Stena Edda and Stena Embla**

All three E-flexer vessels for Stena Line's Irish Sea services are identical and have been given Norse (mythology) names beginning with 'E' which were chosen through a Stena Line employee competition.

*Estrid* is an Old Norse Eastern-Nordic version of the name Astrid. Estrid is commonly found on old runestones and means 'divinely beautiful'.

*Edda* is an old Norse term that refers to a central medieval collection of poems and divine mythology.

*Embla* means 'the first female, created by Gods'.

**Routes**

| | |
|---|---|
| Stena Embla | Holyhead – Dublin |
| Stena Edda | Liverpool (Birkenhead) – Belfast |
| Stena Embla | Liverpool (Birkenhead) – Belfast *from early 2021* |

| | |
|---|---|
| Builder | China Merchants Jinling Shipbuilding, Weihai (formerly AVIC Weihai)) |
| Engines | 2 x Caterpillar MaK 12 M43 C gas ready (Methanol/LNG) V12 4-stroke |
| Propellers | 2 x Wärtsilä Controllable Pitch |
| Fuel | Marine Diesel/LNG |
| Output | 25,200 Kw |
| Range | 6,500 nautical miles |
| Length | 214.5 metres |
| Draft | 6.7 metres |
| Beam (width) | 27.8 metres |
| Gross Tonnage | 41,671 gt |
| Speed | 22 knots (41 kph) |
| Lane Metres | 3,100 |
| Freight vehicles | 210 |
| Cars | 120 |
| Passengers | 1,000 |
| Cabins | 175 |
| Berths | 670 |
| Crew | 73 |
| Port of Registry | Limassol |
| Flag | Cyprus |

**Stena Ro-Ro E-Flexer Summary of Confirmed Orders**

| Yard No | Name | Operator | Intended Route |
|---|---|---|---|
| W0263 | Stena Estrid | Stena Line | Holyhead – Dublin |
| W0264 | Stena Edda | Stena Line | Birkenhead – Belfast |
| W0266 | Stena Embla | Stena Line | Birkenhead – Belfast |
| W0267 | Galicia | Brittany Ferries | Portsmouth – Santander/Bilbao |
| W0268 | Côte d'Opale | DFDS | Dover – Calais |
| W0269 | Salamanca | Brittany Ferries | Portsmouth – Santander/Bilbao |
| W0270 | Santoña | Brittany Ferries | Portsmouth – Santander/Bilbao |
| W0271 | TBC | Stena Line | TBC |
| W0272 | TBC | Stena Line | TBC |

*Yard numbers 271 and 272 are 240 metres long and 45,000gt. Steel cutting for 271 began on 29th May, 2020.*

Another aerial view of the *Stena Estrid* at her fitting out berth, this time from the starboard side. (*CMI Jinling Weihai Shipyard*)

# In New Waters

This stunning image of the *Stena Superfast X* in its new rather garish red livery was taken prior to her being formally renamed as *A Nepita* by Corsica Linea in June 2020 for services between France and Algeria. Her major refit included the installation of scrubbers together with 94 new cabins with a further 33 crew cabins being converted to passenger use. *(George Giannakis)*

In 2011 the Stena Caledonia (ex St David 1981) was withdrawn and sold to PT. ASDP, Indonesia and renamed *Port Link* for services between Merak and Bakauheni. She remains in active service today. *(Author's Collection)*

The *Leif Ericson* was formerly the *Stena Challenger* (1991) until sold to Marine Atlantica (Canada) for delivery in 2001 for services between North Sydney (Nova Scotia), Argentia and Port aux Basques (both Newfoundland) where viewed departing for Nova Scotia). *(Jarrod David)*

The *SNAV Adriatico* is the former *Koningin Beatrix* which served on the Hoek van Holland-Harwich route from 1986 and then Fishguard-Rosslare from 1997 until 2002. Seen here at her home port of Naples, today she operates for Grandi Navi Veloci (GNV) on their service to Palermo. *(Daniel F)*

Sold in February 2002, to International Maritime Transport Corporation (IMTC), Casablanca, Morocco, the S*tena Galloway* (ex *Galloway Princess*) was renamed *Le Rif* for their Algeciras-Tangiers service. Now Africa Morocco Link's *Morocco Sun*, viewed arriving at Algeciras from the new port of Tanger Med.. *(Justo Prieto)*

The *Stena Cambria*'s (ex *St Anselm*) withdrawal from Stena Line service came in early February 1999. Sold to Umafisa, Ibiza, Spain she was renamed I*sla de Botafoc* for their Ibiza-Barcelona route. Today Ventouris Ferries operate her as the *Bari* between there and Durres (Albania). *(Miles Cowsill)*

Withdrawn in late 2011 when the new Loch Ryan Port opened, the *Stena Navigator* (ex *SeaFrance Manet*) dates from 1984. Quickly snapped up she is now Balearia's P*oeta Lopez Anglada* on services from Tanger Med to Algeciras where she was photographed in January 2020. *(Justo Prieto)*

Once the pride of the Sealink fleet and latterly the *Stena Adventurer* (ex *Stena Hibernia*, ex *St Columba 1977*) she was sold in 1997 to Agapitos Express Ferries, Greece becoming their *Express Aphrodite*. Today, she is the *Masarrah* on the pilgrim route across the Red Sea between Safaga and Duba for Namma Shipping Lines. *(Wil Wijsters)*

# Index

# Postscript

The rapid spread of the virulent Covid-19 coronavirus strain in 2020 has had a devastating effect and fast changed our world, providing unprecedented challenges. None more so than on the transport and travel industries, with ferries, cruise ships and aircraft laid up and operators facing major financial difficulties.

Stena Line has not been immune from this and has experienced a significant decline in passenger and freight volumes across all its 20 European routes, resulting in having to either furlough employees or make them redundant.  The company employs about 2,500 people in the United Kingdom and Ireland making more than 250 crossings per week across the Irish Sea, carrying 750,000 freight units annually. Overall, some 80 per cent of Irish exports travel through the three ports Stena Line owns: Holyhead, Fishguard and Cairnryan in Scotland.

The focus for Stena Line was to ensure that essential supply lines stayed operational, carrying both freight and people on essential journeys. Around 65% of all Northern Ireland freight travels on their vessels, with freight traffic down by 30% and passenger figures by over 80%, the number of sailings on offer have been reduced accordingly. Stena Line estimates that passenger figures are unlikely to recover until well into 2021.

In a fast moving and fluid situation with no definite end to the crisis in sight, the future shape and size of the ferry industry in general is full of imponderables, though an increased emphasis on pure ro-ro freight operations may result as producers look for shorter and less vulnerable supply chains.  State support of lifeline operations will need reappraising, to ensure that ferries can confidently continue to operate without the risk of closure if another pandemic or similar occurs. On the passenger side, travel habits may take time to return to something like normality, and certainly not until social distancing restrictions are universally removed. In the more immediate term, the check-in procedures at ferry terminals are likely to be more complex and therefore time-consuming, which may deter casual travellers.

On a more positive note, Stena's resilience has been well documented, the company's diversification has always been their strength. Their new E-Flexer ferries are a prime example of their forward and flexible thinking, further exemplified by the development work their Stena Teknik subsidiary is doing with their advanced, fully-electric ferry Stena Elektra which they hope will be in service by 2030.

Great things therefore still to come from 'the world's leading ferry company'!

Stena Elektra

# Acknowledgements

I am grateful for all the help that has been given in the preparation of this book, especially from Miles Cowsill (Ferry Publications), Matt Davies, Gordon Hislip, and Philippe Holthof for their photographic contributions. Matt also for his article on Stena's new E-Flexer class ferries and general assistance with the text. Richard Kirkman for his excellent map of Stena's Irish Sea routes and Phil Bryant for his meticulous proofing and trying to improve my grammar and punctuation. My thanks as well to all those photographers who have generously allowed the use of their images.

Last, but not least, to my wife Cathy, not just for her proofing contributions, but also for her support and patience during the writing of this book.

Whilst every care has been taken in ascertaining that all images have been correctly accredited feedback is welcomed so as to be able to address any inaccuracies.